How Faith Works

by
Frederick K.C. Price

HARRISON HOUSE
Tulsa, Oklahoma

13th Printing
Over 140,000 in Print

ISBN 0-89274-001-9

Printed in United States of America

Table of Contents

Foreword

I travel a lot all over the country.
(The Lord has thrust me into a ministry of
teaching, primarily in the area of faith.)
And I find that 9 out of 10 people don't know
what faith is. I'd almost go so far as to say
9 and 9/10 percent of every 10 people don't know
what faith is.

WHAT IS FAITH, ANYWAY?

First, the study of faith is very important
to YOU.

Without faith—you can't please God. (Hebrews 11:6)

Without faith—you'll never get your prayers answered.

Without understanding the principles of faith—you'll
never be able to live in full continuous victory,
spiritually as a Christian.

Part I

FAITH AND BELIEF:
Are they the same?

1

FAITH IS...
one side of a coin

There are two words used throughout the Scriptures which are always used separately and independently. Yet in the natural—or in everyday life—we tend to make those two words synonymous terms. They are different words—spelled differently, pronounced differently—yet we make both words mean the same thing in our lives and in our actions.

The words are: *faith* and *belief.*

Most people think *faith* and *belief* are the same thing. Most people think *believing is faith,* and *faith is believing.* Most people think, "If I believe, that's faith," and, "If I have faith, that means I believe."

I thought that myself. For 17 years as a minister of the gospel, I thought *to believe* was *to have faith.* And I thought *to have faith* was *to believe.* I operated on that premise. And I was defeated in my life.

I was a Christian. My name was written in the Lamb's Book of Life. Had I dropped dead at any point, I would have gone to heaven. No question about it.

But in terms of the everyday, I didn't have victory in my life. I was frustrated. In debt. In bondage. Fearful of one thing and then the other. My prayers weren't really being answered.

Oh, I would pray and go through the motions. But if I got 5 prayers answered in 15 years, I don't know about it. I was just going through it and doing something because I'd heard somebody else do it that way. But in terms of knowing—*The specific things I asked for, did I get them?*—if I got them 5 times in 15 years, I don't know about it.

I thought that because I believed God's Word—I believed the Bible was the Word of God—that meant I was exercising faith. But, I wasn't.

Faith and *belief* are two sides to the same coin.

In the natural, in our economy, we have coins—dimes, nickels, quarters, half-dollars, silver dollars. These coins have two sides. One side is referred to as the heads side. (It usually has the head of a person, a president, etc., on it.) And the other side we call the tails side. It's common usage—heads and tails.

In our natural economy, in order to use a coin as legal tender, as an instrument of barter in purchasing goods and services, both sides of that coin must be intact. If one side is defaced and marred, and the individual to whom you give the coin sees it, he will not accept that coin as legal tender. It's not legally good if one side is marred. You have to have both sides intact in order for the coin to be legal tender.

In the realm of the spirit, it is the same. *Faith* and *belief* are two sides to the same coin. If one of those sides, the heads or the tails, is not intact, it won't spend. It won't work.

Let me show you clearly the difference between *faith* and *belief*. Because if you don't know the difference, you'll never truly be able to exercise faith.

You'll think you're exercising faith—but you won't be. It's important to know when you're exercising faith. You should know it with all the assurance that you know whether you're male or female.

How long does it take you to answer a form question as to whether you are a male or a female? Not long, does it? You ought to know that. If you don't know it, you're in serious trouble. You ought to know whether you're male or female.

Well, how do you know? Do you have to say, "Let me see. I'd better pray about it and see if I can get a confirmation. Maybe somebody will prophesy over me and tell me . . ."?

No! You ought to know. You ought to be able to say, "I'm a man, a male. I have all the standard equipment to prove it." Or, "I'm a woman, a female. I have the standard equipment to prove it."

You need to be that certain about faith. You ought to know, that you know, that you know, that you know, that you're exercising faith. God doesn't expect us to walk in the dark. He expects us to walk in faith.

Now let me show you the difference between faith and believing, for they are not the same. I'll prove it to you. I want you to visualize. Use your imagination . . .

A man staggers through the door . . . over to a chair . . . prepares to sit down at a table . . . BUT INSTEAD, HE FALLS ONTO THE FLOOR.

Several people rush to his side . . . They pick him up . . . and set him in the chair. He seems to be out of it.

They fan him . . . wake him up . . . and say, "Brother, what's the matter? What's the matter with you?"

Groggily and weakly he answers, "Ah . . . I don't know. I don't know."

Somebody says, "I wonder if there's a doctor in this motel?"

The group calls the desk. Sure enough there happens to be a doctor in the motel.

The doctor enters and makes a preliminary examination of the man.

THE DOCTOR: "This man is in the final stages of starvation. This man is suffering from malnutrition. He's almost dead. Given another 30 minutes—all things being equal—this man will be dead. He's starving to death."

The leaders get together and say, "Let's go down to the kitchen and see if we can get the chef to prepare some food for this man. We certainly don't want him to starve to death."

They enter later with a four-wheeler, loaded down with all kinds of good food.

They wheel it up to the man and say, "Brother, do you see this food?"

And he says, "Yes."

"All right," they say, "do you believe that if you eat this food it will keep you from starving to death?"

And he says, "Oh, yes."

They say again, "Do you believe that if you eat this food it will keep you from starving to death?"

And again he says, "Oh yes, certainly I believe that if I eat that food it will keep me from starving to death."

Then he says it again, "I believe that if I eat this food it will keep me from starving to death . . . I believe that if I eat this food, it will keep me from starving to death . . . I believe that if I eat this food it will keep me from starving to death."

(Now remember, the doctor had given him 30 minutes to live.)

So . . . 29 minutes and 50 seconds later . . . the man is heard to say, "I believe that if I eat this food, it will keep me from starving to d

    e

      a

        t

          h

            .

              . . .

He falls to the floor.

The doctor rushes to his side and says, "This man is dead."

I have a question for you. The man said with his own mouth that he believed if he ate the food, it would keep him from starving to death. My question is: Was that true?

The man said, "I believe that if I eat that food it will keep me from starving to death." Was what the man said true? Was it true?

The man died with food in view. And he said with his mouth that he believed if he ate the food, it would keep him from starving to death. Yet he died.

Why did he die? *Because he didn't eat it!*

What he believed was true. Scientifically and historically it is a proven fact—all things being equal—that if you eat food you won't die from starvation. You may die from snake bite. But you won't die from starving to death, if you eat food.

The man believed that. Everything he believed was absolutely, positively, unequivocally true—yet he died!

Why? He died because he didn't eat the food. The eating of the food is faith! *Faith is acting on what you believe.*

FAITH IS . . .

acting on what you believe

If you don't act on what you believe, you'll die just like the man in our illustration died. That's why thousands and thousands of Christians, who were prayed for as they lay in hospitals—lovely Christians, who loved the Lord, whose names were written in the Lamb's Book of Life, who spoke in tongues—yet they died. Thank God they died and went to heaven. But they died on that bed believing that God could heal them, just as that man believed if he ate the food it would keep him from starving to death. But he still died.

Everything he believed was true. But it didn't do him any *personal* good. It did him no *personal* good, even though what he believed was true.

Do you see it? That's the difference between *believing* and *faith*.

You can believe all day long—and still die. You can believe God can heal you—and still die of cancer. And still die of a heart condition. And still die of some other ailment.

You can believe, and everything you believe can be absolutely, documentarily true, you can prove it by the Word of God. But until you start doing something about what you believe, it's not faith. It's only belief. And you won't get anything just believing. That's the difference— and it's an important difference.

Most people believe. They'll say, "Oh, I know the Lord can heal me . . . if it's His will . . . in His own good time."

You won't get healed on that.

"Well, I know God can supply my needs. I know He's able to do it. I believe He's able."

You'll still go to the poor farm. Believing won't get it.

You have to do more than believe. Whatever you do—how you act—is certainly based on what you believe. They go together. You can't act unless you have some knowledge. And you can't have knowledge without believing in that knowledge, otherwise you wouldn't act on it. But you have not only *to believe* a thing, you have also *to do* something about what you believe before what you believe will affect you in a personal way.

What you believe may be true. Just as what the man believed was true. We couldn't fault his believing. But it didn't help him, did it? He died. Why did he die? Because he did not act on what he believed. He had to eat it before it would do him any personal good. And that action— the eating—that's what faith is.

2

FAITH IS ...

a working principle in two realms

Faith is the same in the spirit realm as it is in the natural realm. The difference between the two realms is that the spiritual realm is the Heavenly Father's realm, and the natural realm is Satan's realm. Faith, however, works the same way in either realm. The principle is the same.

In our natural economy, 2 and 2 is 4 at the meat market . . . 2 and 2 is 4 at the vegetable stand . . . 2 and 2 is 4 at the new car dealer . . . 2 and 2 is 4 at the bank. In our society, no matter what you're dealing in—services, goods, or whatever—the principle is the same. Whether you're buying a Bible or the latest paperback, the principle is the same.

Faith is faith—whether it's in the natural realm or the spiritual realm. And faith in both realms is based upon something which you believe. And what you believe is based on something you have been told by word of mouth, the written page, or in some other form.

Here's how faith works in the natural realm. 1) You are given information. 2) You believe that information. 3) You act on it. Let me illustrate.

Have you ever worked on a 40-hour-a-week job?

When you applied for the job you probably filled out an application, had an interview, and then they hired you. Right? That's usually how it goes.

When you went in the personnel man said something like, "We'll hire you to be an XB operator. We'll pay you

$5 an hour. You'll work 40 hours a week. And paydays are on Friday."

You say, "Goody-goody!"

And he says, "Report to Mr. Bozo in the Bla-Bla Department Monday morning at 8 o'clock."

You run home and tell your wife, or your husband, or your mother, or your father, or your friends, or whomever, "I got a job! I got a job!"

And bright and early Monday morning—in fact you could hardly sleep Sunday night for thinking about getting up Monday morning and going to that new job—you go down there.

You work 8 hours Monday . . . 8 hours Tuesday . . . 8 hours Wednesday . . . 8 hours Thursday . . . 8 hours Friday.

Come Friday evening at the close of the day and you're ready for your paycheck! Right?

Let me ask you this question: What guarantee do you have that you're going to get paid?

No, you don't get it just because you worked for it. In the middle of the week the man who owns the company could have drawn all the money out of the bank and gone to South America. People have done things like that before and the workers didn't get paid. So don't think that just because you work, you get paid.

You get paid . . . and you work . . . *because the man told you you'd get paid.* You acted on his word.

I've worked quite a few years on various jobs, and I've never yet been able to persuade an employer to pay me for 40 hours work before I worked the 40 hours. Maybe you have. But I've never persuaded them.

They always tell me, "You work the 40 hours, Fred, and then we'll pay you."

So—I'm working on the word of a man. I have no other guarantee that I'm going to get paid the amount I was told I'd get paid, other than the fact that the man told me. And I acted on that man's word.

I doubt seriously if you ever hired in on a job and took with you a court order from the Supreme Court and a certified public accountant to examine the books to see if the company had enough money to pay you at the end of 40 hours. You just accepted what the man said. You acted on what he said. You might even have gone out and spent the last money you had buying clothes so you'd be presentable the first day on the job.

You did all that based on words. You acted on the man's word. That was faith in the natural realm. You acted. And the thing about it is, you acted on the man's word when you might not even have known the man's middle initial! You probably had never seen the man before in your entire life. And you know he's a human. He's subject to error. Yet you acted on that man's word, without question!

You didn't argue, "Are you sure you're going to pay me on Friday? Are you positive you'll be able to pay me after 40 hours?"

Did you do that? No! You just accepted his word.

But when it comes to the Lord, you have to have a chicken crow at 3 o'clock in the afternoon, or somebody to prophesy over you to confirm that the Lord meant what He said when He said it. You have to have a sign.

The word of a man you'll swallow hook, line, sinker, fishing pole, reel, fisherman and his boots. You'll swallow the whole thing and never question it.

But when it comes to the Heavenly Father—who hung the sun, the moon, the stars, and created the universe—you want Him to give you a sign before you're ready to act on it.

"Well, I'm not going to believe that I'm healed until I feel the pain leave. How do I know I'm really healed? I still have the pain. I'm not going to say that I believe that I'm healed when I still have the pain."

The doctor can come in after the operation, touch you around where the bandages are—while you're still sore —and say, "According to your chart and all the tests, you're doing fine. You'll be out of here in three days."

And when your relatives come in that night and ask how you're doing, you say, "I'm doing fine. I'll be home in three days."

You still have the pain, but you don't still say you're sick.

But when it comes to God, you're still claiming you're sick even though His Word says that by His stripes you were healed. (I Peter 2:24)

You say you believe His Word. If you believe but you're not acting on it, God's Word will never do you any personal good.

Suppose you applied for a job on Friday. And the personnel man told you the job was yours and to come in on Monday, and that after you'd worked 40 hours you would be paid on Friday. Then all weekend you sit on your couch in front of the big window looking out over the street and say, "Praise God, I have a job. I have a job. I have a job." Then all the next week, you sit on the same couch, looking out the same window, and say the same thing, "I have a job. Isn't it wonderful. I have a job." When Friday comes you won't be paid, because you didn't act —you didn't work.

You can say, "Oh, I believe the Bible. I believe it's the Word of God. There are 39 books in the Old Testament, 27 in the New Testament, and 66 in both of them. Praise the Lord."

But that won't get you a thing, personally. You can believe all day long that the Bible is true—and that's to your credit—but what the Bible says will never affect your life in a personal way until you start acting on God's Word. Even though the Bible is true, it won't do you any personal good until you act on it.

Do you own an automobile? Then you carry the keys in your pocket or purse.

Do you believe that key will start your car? You do? That's true. It will.

But do you know what you could do? You could go out to where the car is parked, sit down on the hood where you could pray, fast, cry, beat on the hood—and the car still wouldn't start.

You could hold the key up to everyone who walks by and stand up and say, "This is the key to the ignition. This is the key that will start the car and I can go home."

But you will sit out there until it snows—all things being equal—and you'll never get home. Until what? Until you act on what you believe.

You'll have to take that key and put it in the ignition. The key won't do it by itself. Just having the key is not enough. You have to put it into the lock and turn it before the car will start.

God's Word is the key. But it will do you about as much good as the key to your car until you put it into the lock of life—into the circumstances of life—and turn it. Everything in it is true. (Just as the key to your car is true—it's the key designed to start your car, but it won't until you put it in.) You can believe God's Word is the key. But until you act on it, it will never do you any personal good.

3

FAITH IS . . .

evidence of the unseen

*Now faith is
the substance of things hoped for,
the evidence of things not seen.*
—Hebrews 11:1

"*Now faith is the SUBSTANCE of things hoped for.* . . . Hope has no substance to it. Hope is a dream. Hope is just an idle thought. It has no tangibility. Substance means that which has materiality. Hope has none. "I hope some day to be rich." That has no tangibility. It's just a dream. Just a figment of my mind. What faith does is give hope substance. Faith gives hope materiality. Faith gives hope tangibility. Faith gives hope substance.

For instance, I'm sick. The doctor says it is a congenital disease. A chronic thing. I'll have it all my life. There's nothing else I can do. I'm born with it. I have to live with it. I can hope to be well. I can see myself running and playing. Walking on my own two feet with no assistance. I can hope for that. But it doesn't have any substance. There is no reality to that hope. I can take *faith*, however, and give my hope *substance* with the Word of God!

"*Now faith is the substance of THINGS hoped for* . . . ." Things. T-h-i-n-g-s. Things. Not ideas. Faith is the substance of things hoped for.

"*Now faith is . . . the evidence of things not seen.*" Faith has only to do with what you don't see. Any time you see anything—and when I say "see," I mean to perceive through your five senses—absolutely no faith is involved. Hebrews 11:1 says that faith is the evidence of things not seen.

Let's say I'm standing before a group of people, and you are one of those people. I hold up my watch in plain view of all and ask, "How many of you can see this watch in my hand?"

How much faith is needed to see the watch?

None.

Why?

Because it can be seen.

But if I should hold both hands behind my back and say, "I have a watch in my right hand," now it can't be seen.

You have nothing to go on but my word. You can either believe my word or disbelieve my word. Now *faith* has to be the *evidence* of the thing you *don't see.* And your faith has to be in my word. It's all you have to go on.

You could say, "I don't believe Price is telling the truth. I think he's lying. He doesn't have a watch." And you could go on your way.

Or, you could say, "I believe it."

Someone walks up to you and says, "Hey, what do you think about that Fred Price saying he has a watch behind his back. Do you believe that?"

"Yes sir," you say, "I believe it. He gave me his word on it. I'm acting like it's so."

You can't see the watch now, so you have to use faith. And your faith has to be in my word. For it is impossible for you to use faith until you have some knowledge. And you can't have knowledge until somebody gives it to you. They have to give it to you by word of mouth, by the printed page, etc. In some way you must receive knowledge that the watch is there. Only then can you believe or disbelieve.

"Now faith is . . . the evidence of things not seen." What a marvelous statement! Faith is the evidence! Faith is the evidence of things! Of things! Of things not seen! Not seen! Faith is the evidence of things not seen!

Do you know what the word "evidence" means? Evidence is that which supports the existence of something. Or—that which supports the fact a thing exists.

If I have evidence of something, that means I don't have the thing. But, I have some substantial substance which shows that thing exists. Evidence proves the existence of something else. Right?

Notice it says that faith is the evidence of things not seen. You would have a tendency, in the natural, to think that because you can't see a thing it doesn't exist. But this verse says that faith is the evidence of the thing you don't see.

If faith is the evidence, then the thing—though not seen—must be real. If it were not real, faith couldn't be the evidence. Faith can't be the evidence of something which doesn't exist. Even though I don't see it, it must still exist. Because if it didn't exist in reality, faith could not be the evidence for it. You can't have evidence for something which doesn't exist—can you? Faith is the evidence of things not seen.

II CORINTHIANS 4:18
18 While we look not at the things which are seen, but at the things which are not seen: for the things which are seen are temporal; but the things which are not seen are eternal.

"*While we look not at the things which are seen* . . ." Which are seen.

". . . *but at the things* . . ." Things. T-h-i-n-g-s.

". . . *which are not seen* . . ." Not seen.

". . . *for the things which are seen are temporal;* . . ." Or, temporary.

". . . *but the things which are not seen are eternal.*"

That sounds almost ridiculous. How in the world can you look at something that's not seen?

Only with the eye of faith!

Paul wrote here, "*While we* . . ." The "we" refers to those of us in the Body of Christ.

He said, "*While we look not* . . ." In other words, we don't look at the things which are seen. We don't make our value judgments based on what we see.

I don't say I'm sick because I feel sick. I don't say my needs are not met because I don't see the money. If

I'm walking in line with God's Word, I find the Word of God which promises me my well-being, my healing, or my needs, etc. Then I say, "According to the Word of God . . ." And the Word of God becomes my evidence. I believe that and act on it. Then faith becomes my evidence of the thing not seen. Faith is what causes the unseen thing to come into visibility.

II CORINTHIANS 5:7
7 (For we walk by faith, not by sight:)

What's he talking about, *"We walk by faith, not by sight"*?

That means that the man of God—the Christian—walks by faith. He doesn't walk by what he sees. He doesn't make judgments nor base his actions on what he sees. He bases his actions on what *"thus saith the Lord"*.

Therefore you can see how important it is to know what *"thus saith the Lord"*. If you don't know what the Word of God says on the issue you need help on, you won't be able to exercise any faith. It is absolutely impossible to do it.

If you don't know the Word of God promises you healing, there's no way in the world you can believe for healing. Not by faith. Now if God desires to do it by the sovereign grace work of the Holy Spirit—such as in the Kathryn Kuhlman type meetings—you might get healed. The only sad thing about that is, you can't be guaranteed you will be the one healed. And if the doctor has given you only 6 months to live—buddy, you don't have time to play Russian roulette. You'd better know that you have something that's going to work.

Paul said, *"We walk by faith. . . ."* That means we walk by the Word of God.

Then what does the Word of God have to say about my physical well-being? What does God's Word have to say about my prayer life? What does God's Word say about my needs being met? I have to find the Word of God on these things, and then act on that Word instead of on what I see.

God's Word says, *"While we look not at the things which are seen, but at the things which are not seen: . . ."* We don't look at the things which are seen.

I don't look at the cancer. I don't look at the tumor. I don't look at anything in the natural. All that is in the natural. It's not in the Word of God.

If I expect to receive what the Word of God says about it, I can't look at the natural and make my value judgment on that saying, "I'm sick." Because when I say that, I've signed for the package. I have taken authority for it, and it belongs to me legally. Satan can enforce it upon my body. And he will kill me with it. In fact—if you let him—he'll kill you with a broken toenail. He wants you dead. And he'll kill you with a split hair if you let him.

"We walk by faith, not by sight." That means I walk by what the Word of God says. So I must know what it says before I can walk by it. That's where many get bogged down. They go to meetings and sit there with their arms folded. They don't have a Bible. They just sit there listening—but hearing nothing. In one ear and out the other. And they're the ones repeatedly coming up in need of prayer, the ones continually sending in prayer requests.

The key is God's Word. But I have to know what the keys fit. When I find out what the keys fit and start applying those keys, I'll start walking in the fullness of God. I'll start walking in the fullness of what's been provided for me through Christ in His redemptive work at Calvary. I have to know how to use my faith. And I have to know what faith is.

The Unseen

"Now faith is the substance of things hoped for, the evidence of things NOT SEEN."

Did you know *unseen* things are more real—or actually *spiritual* things are more real—than physical things?

Do you know why? Spiritual things existed before any material thing ever existed.

Jesus said, in talking to the woman at the well in Samaria,*"God is a Spirit."* (John 4:24)

He didn't say God is spirit. He didn't say God is mind. He didn't say God is a mind. He said God is a Spirit—a Spirit—separate and distinct from other spirit beings.

Do you know why? Because angels are spirits. Satan is a spirit. Demons are spirits. *And you are a spirit.*

You don't have one. You are one. You are a spirit —you have a soul—and you live in a body. You don't have a spirit, you are a spirit. The real you is a spirit man.

That's what the Bible means when it says we are made in the image of God. God is a Spirit. Man is made like God. Man is a spirit. Animals were not made spiritual beings. They have only flesh and souls. They don't have spirits.

Jesus said that God is a Spirit. And the Bible says in the Book of Genesis that God created the heaven and the earth. Right? The heavens and the earth are physical, tangible things. God had to exist before He could create the heavens and the earth. So if God, who is a Spirit, existed before the heavens and the earth were created, that means spiritual things are more real than physical things. It took spiritual things to create physical things. God existed first. Then He, by His existence, brought the material things into manifestation. So actually, spiritual things are more real than physical things.

EPHESIANS 1:3
3 Blessed be the God and Father of our Lord Jesus Christ, who hath blessed us with all spiritual blessings in heavenly places in Christ:

"Blessed be the God and Father of our Lord Jesus Christ, who hath. . ." "Hath" is an Old English word for our present day word "has," which you realize is a past tense term. It indicates the time of the action has already taken place. So what it's saying here is, God has already done this that Paul is talking about. It's already an accom-

plished fact as far as God is concerned.

Listen to what it says, *"Blessed be the God and Father of our Lord Jesus Christ, WHO HATH. . . ."* It didn't say, Who's *going to bless.* It didn't say, He's thinking about blessing. It didn't say, He's taking it under consideration. It says, *". . . who hath blessed us. . . ."* Who *HAS* blessed us! I'm already blessed!

What has He blessed me with?

" . . . with all. . . ." With *All!* Not with some. But with *ALL!*

All what?

". . . ALL SPIRITUAL BLESSINGS IN HEAVENLY PLACES. . . ."

Somebody says, "Yes, Brother Price, but that's just it. I need a new car—that's not spiritual. I need a new job—that's not spiritual. I need some more clothes—that's not spiritual."

Wait a minute. You're missing it. All things are first of all spiritual, then they become physical. Even a car, a house, a dress, first of all existed in the mind of the designer before ever being produced.

Consider a skyscraper, for instance. Workers don't just come out to the site with a bunch of dump trucks and rocks and say, "Let's put up a building," then start dumping stuff out on the ground. No. Some men come and measure the land. Blueprints and drawings are made. They make an artist's conception of what it will look like when it's finished. All this takes place before they ever start working on it, before they ever break ground. The idea for the building was in the mind of a man before it ever became a building.

Everything is first of all in the mind of God, before it becomes a physical manifestation. So when it says, *". . . who hath blessed us with all spiritual blessings. . . .",* that means everything you need—including things tangible and material—to make your life a success is already in the Bank of Heaven. It's already in God. He has already blessed you with it. He put it on your account. What you have to do is start writing checks on it. Then it becomes yours experientially.

You could have a million dollars deposited in the bank in your account. You could be given the passbook and the checkbook. But if you don't write some checks, you'll never get the benefit of the money.

It's all in the Bank of Heaven. Faith is the way you write checks to draw it out. Legally, it belongs to you. His Word says He has already blessed you with it. If He didn't want you to have it, why did He bless you with it?

It's already there. "... *who hath. ...*" Hath. Has. Not, He's going to. Not, He's thinking about it. But, *Who HAS BLESSED US with all spiritual blessings.*

That covers every need you can think of—plus your desires. When you're walking in line with the perfect will of God—meaning when your heart's desire is to do the will of the Lord—you can have the very desires of your heart. (See Psalm 37:4.) Because when you're walking in line with the Word of God, wanting and desiring to do the perfect will of God, you won't ask for any dumb, stupid thing that would take you away from God.

So get off that kick about, "Well, the Lord knows if you get this new Cadillac, you would probably turn away from the church, so He doesn't let you have it."

That's garbage. It's an excuse Satan has used to keep the church poor. Having things is not what keeps you away from God—*IT'S THINGS HAVING YOU.*

The Bible says, *"For the love of money is the root of all evil. ..."*

People misquote it and say, "You know, honey, the Bible says that money is the root of all evil."

It doesn't say that at all. It says, "... *the love of money. ...*" Having the money is not the point. It's the loving of it. You can love it and not have a dime. That's why people rob banks—they don't have any money and they love it, and they're trying to get it for nothing.

The Lord has never been opposed to your having things. He's always been opposed to things having you. That was the rich young ruler's problem. Some people have taken that account and used it as a reason for Christians being poor.

The Bible says of the rich young ruler who came to Jesus that he had great possessions. Jesus said, *". . . sell all that thou hast, and distribute unto the poor, and thou shalt have treasure in heaven: and come, follow me"* (Luke 18:22).

He didn't do it. Why? Because he loved those possessions.

He wanted eternal life. Jesus didn't go to him. He came to Jesus and asked, *"Good Master, what shall I do to inherit eternal life?"* (Luke 18:18).

Jesus said, "Keep the commandments."

He said, "I've done those."

Jesus said, "One thing thou lackest. Sell everything. Give it to the poor. And follow me."

But the Bible says he went away sorrowful. Why? Because he had great possessions. Actually it should have been written, great possessions had him.

Jesus wasn't opposed to money. It takes money to build churches. It takes money to print books. It takes money to send missionaries around the world. To establish churches. God couldn't possibly be opposed to money.

You couldn't get the gospel preached if it weren't for money. You can't get radio time without money. You can't get on television without money.

It's not the money. It's not the thing. It's when the thing has you—when it becomes your God. That's why Jesus told him to give it away. The things had him. To show you how much those possessions did have him, he couldn't get rid of them. He couldn't give them up.

I'm thoroughly convinced in my own heart that if the man had been willing to give it all away, the Lord would have said, "Keep it." Because can you imagine what God could do if Howard Hughes would be converted? Four billion dollars spending change! That's not considering the million dollar hotels, his assets, his oil wells. That's just his mad money. Four billion dollars! Oh, how that could help the cause of Christ. Think how much prime time we could buy with four billion dollars to preach the gospel on TV.

Instead, much of the church is going around begging, selling barbecue dinners on Saturday afternoons because we're so poor. We've had this poverty syndrome drilled into us all our lives. Raffles and bazaars. Chicken dinners and pie sales. To raise money for the Kingdom of God! The Creator of the universe! And the best He can do is get some chicken dinners to help Him out. It's pitiful. A disgrace before God.

What God could do with some sanctified millions!

He's not opposed to your having things. He doesn't care if you have a Cadillac to drive on Monday, a Rolls Royce for Tuesday, a Mercedes Benz on Wednesday, a Jaguar on Thursday, a Thunderbird on Friday, and an El Dorado on Saturday. It doesn't make Him any difference. He doesn't have to ride in it. He doesn't have to put gas in it, keep the windshields wiped, the tires up, and the thing washed. That's your problem, not His. It doesn't matter to Him what you have. But when things start getting hold of you, that's what's dangerous. And you can let stuff get hold of you when you don't have a crying dime.

It's not the *things*. After all, who made the gold? Wasn't it God? Do you mean to tell me He made it for Satan and his children? Who made the oil? Did He make it for Satan and his kids? They seem to have most of it. The church sure doesn't have any. Do you know any churches that have oil wells? Maybe you do. I'd like to meet the members.

Most Christians I know don't have very much. They're on the bread line, on the county, looking for a handout from the city, or something like that. Too many of them at least.

Begging and whining, "I don't know if we're gonna be able to stay on the air," talking about a faith ministry. "We're just about at that point in the summertime when everybody goes on vacation, and our offerings are coming in very slowly. If you want this broadcast to stay on the air, send your offerings in immediately. We really need your help."

Isn't that pitiful?

We've been on two radio stations, thirty minutes a day, for four years. And we've paid our radio time in advance the entire four years. I've never asked for one dime, or nickel, or penny on that broadcast. God meets all the needs according to His riches in glory by Christ Jesus. Our radio cost is about $1,000 a month—$12,000 to $13,000 a year for four years. All paid in advance. Without asking for a penny. We don't have to.

I don't have to get on in the summer talking about, "Things are getting bad now. You'd better send us some money."

The Word of God says, *"But my God shall supply all your needs according to his riches in glory by Christ Jesus" (Philippians 4:19).* It doesn't say He will supply according to *YOUR POVERTY*, but according *to HIS RICHES!* Praise God! He's rich!

". . . Who hath blessed us with all spiritual blessings. . . ." Remember that everything physical first of all was spiritual. God, who is a Spirit, created all physical things. And according to Hebrews 11:1, faith is the evidence of those things we don't see.

The Things

Now what are the *things?*

The *things* are recorded in the New Covenant. I have to get into the New Covenant and find out what the New Covenant says about it.

I wouldn't argue with a person five minutes about whether or not it's God's will for every Christian to be well. Yet you hear people with all kinds of con stories talking about, "Well, you know the Lord, it's His will for you to be sick. He's making a better person out of you," and all that kind of garbage. It turns my stomach when I hear it. It's ignorance. Ignorance of God's Word.

Go to the Bible. What does God say about it?

The Word of God says, *". . . Himself took our infirmities, and bare our sicknesses"* (Matthew 8:17). Why did He take them and bear them if He wants me to take them and bear them? It's stupid for both of us to carry them.

And then I Peter 2:24 says, *"Who his own self bare our sins in his own body on the tree, that we, being dead to sins, should live unto righteousness: by whose stripes ye were healed".* YE WERE HEALED! Not, You're going to be. But, You were healed.

"How come I'm sick?" you might ask.

Because you're saying that you're sick. The Word of God says that you're well. But as long as you take sides against the Word of God, the Word of God can't work on your behalf.

When you start to get in line with the Word and say, "Praise God, according to the Word of God, with His stripes I was healed," sickness and disease will flee your home, your premises, and your body. It will not be able to stay there.

"Then how come so many Christians are sick, Brother Price? How come so many good Christians die with sickness and disease?"

It's because they didn't know their rights in Christ. And Satan—the con man—will rob you just like a con man in the natural will take you for your money if you don't know your rights. Satan has robbed us. It doesn't mean they weren't Christians. It doesn't mean they didn't love the Lord. It doesn't mean their names weren't written in the Lamb's Book of Life. It doesn't mean they didn't go to heaven when they died. What it means is they were robbed and cheated out of many fruitful years they could have had in this life.

And then how pitiful to use that old stuff about, "It was the Lord's will to take So-and-so from the earthly realm up to His heavenly garden. He took him up there to the heavenly place to be with Him in His heavenly home."

Why? What for? He has 50 billion angels up there to do His bidding. He doesn't need to take you up there to do something for Him. He can't count on you anyhow. But the angels will do whatever He wants quicker than you can snap your finger.

What would He need you there for? There aren't any sinners up there who need to hear the Word to get saved. There are no sick people to lay hands on. No demons to cast out. What would He need you there for? The battle is down here. The people in bondage are down here. Nobody's in bondage in heaven. There's no sickness and disease up in heaven. No fear. The battle is down here. The captives are down here. And they need to be set free!

No! It's to God's advantage for you to live 500 years if you can!

And don't give me that junk about, "Well, when So-and-so died her husband who would never go to church finally got saved. And his brother got saved. And someone else got saved. In all, three people got saved as a result."

Praise the Lord they got saved. But she didn't have to die for them to get saved. Jesus died 1900 years ago. That's all they needed to get saved. They were probably just too hardheaded and ornery to accept it before that. But don't credit it to the fact that she died.

Just think about it. If she died at 30 and 3 people got saved as a result of her dying at 30—suppose she'd lived out the full life we've been promised, which is at least 70 years. That would have meant 40 more years. If she did no more than convince or influence one person a year for the next 40 years, that would have been 37 more people than the 3 who were saved when she died.

"Now faith is the substance of things hoped for, the evidence of things not seen."

Things exist in two forms—first in their spiritual form, then in their material form. Faith is simply bringing what is invisible into visibility. Why? Because faith is the evidence of things not seen. If the things were not real and did not exist somewhere, faith couldn't be their evidence. You can't have evidence for things which do not exist.

An exciting revelation from the Old Testament brings out in bold relief the fact of things existing in two forms.

In II Kings, Chapter 6, the king of Syria warred against the nation of Israel.

Every time the children of Israel went out to do battle, the Syrians would plan an ambush to waylay them. But every time they planned an ambush, the king of Israel would know about it, because there was a prophet in Samaria named Elisha.

Elisha was anointed by the Spirit of God to stand in the office of a prophet. Therefore, he had the *word of knowledge* at work in his ministry. (I Corinthians 12:8)

By the word of knowledge Elisha would always know about the ambush plans of the Syrians. He would tell the king of Israel. The king of Israel would ambush the ambush. And Israel would always come out on top.

Finally the king of Syria said, "Man, we must have a fink in the ranks. Somebody is snitching on us. They're telling all our plans. We must have a traitor in our midst."

One of his men said, "Oh no, King, there is a prophet over in Samaria who knows everything."

(In reality Elisha didn't know everything just because he was a prophet. He would only know what God revealed to him.)

"Where is he?" the king of Syria asked.

"He's over in the city of Dothan."

"All right," the king said, "get the regiments together. We're going over there and we're going to kill him."

The Syrians came to Dothan and surrounded the city.

Elisha had a servant, Gehazi. Gehazi went out early one morning to draw some water. He decided to walk around the wall. And when he looked over into the valley he saw all the Syrians. It scared him! It blew his mind!

He ran back to Elisha crying, "My master, my master, how shall we do? How shall we do? The army of the Syrians! The army of the Syrians!"

The prophet, just waking up and stretching, said, "What's on your mind, brother?"

"Sir, the army of the Syrians has the city surrounded. They're going to do us in."

The prophet dressed and said, "Show me what you're talking about."

They went out to the wall and looked over.

"See! See!" Gehazi said. "The whole valley is full of the army of the Syrians."

And here is what Elisha said:

II KINGS 6:16
16 And he answered, Fear not: for they that be with us are more than they that be with them.

Picture it. Here is the young man, Gehazi. He has just looked over the wall. He's seen all the soldiers, thousands of them. The whole valley is full of them. And he hears the prophet say, "There are more with us than be with them."

Gehazi starts counting. Looking into the valley he counts, "Five thousand, ten thousand, fifteen thousand, twenty thousand . . ." Then he looks at Elisha and himself, "One, two."

He couldn't get hold of it. He couldn't put a handle on it. "This guy has flipped out," he thought. It must be too early in the morning for him."

Now read verse 17:

II KINGS 6:17a
17 And Elisha prayed, and said, LORD, I pray thee, open his eyes, that he may see . . ."

Wait a minute. That sounds like a contradictory statement. The young man already has his eyes open. He was looking over the wall. That's what scared him—what he saw. So he must have had his eyes open. He saw the army of the Syrians, that's what blew his mind. He was frightened because of what he saw. And here the prophet's praying, "Lord, open his eyes." His eyes are already open.

Ah! . . . But Elisha was talking about something else. He was talking about the eyes of the man who lives on the inside—*the real man*—the real you. He was talking about the eyes of the spirit, your spiritual eyes.

Here's the rest of verse 17:

II KINGS 6:17b
17 . . . And the LORD opened the eyes of the

young man; and he saw: and, behold, the mountain was full of horses and chariots of fire round
about Elisha.

Now here is the revelation. Don't you realize that
before that young man's eyes could be opened to see the
chariots and the horses, the chariots and the horses had to
have already existed?

They were already there before his eyes were opened. Just because he couldn't physically see them didn't
mean they weren't there. They were there all the time.
Elisha saw it and knew it. And when Gehazi's eyes were
opened, he saw the horses and chariots of fire. But the
horses and chariots already existed. If they didn't already
exist, when his eyes were opened he would not have
seen them.

This scripture shows us that things exist in that spirit
world. It is faith which brings them into this physical
world.

"Now faith is . . . the evidence of things not seen."
Faith is the evidence of things not seen. Faith, in other
words, proves that the things exist.

4

FAITH ISN'T . . .

based on experience

Faith is not belief. Belief is not faith. But faith is based on what you believe. The Christian's believing should be based on what is written in the Word and not what someone has experienced.

I don't base anything on experience.

"But what about so-and-so . . . and so-and-so . . . ?"

Don't tell me about it. I don't want to hear it. Don't tell me about somebody you knew who was a Christian who was sick and died. I don't want to hear about it.

It's sad they died. But God's Word told me that we ". . . *walk by faith, not by sight*" (II Corinthians 5:7). This means we walk by the Word of God and not by experiences.

You don't know what people are believing. I've ministered to people and learned later they didn't even believe what I was talking about. And I thought they did. They were standing there saying, "I believe, I believe, I agree, I agree," and come to find out later they weren't agreeing at all. They were believing in something else.

You can't afford to go by experiences. Don't do it! Go by what the Word of God says. Find out what the

Word of God says about your need, or your physical condition—then accept that! Act on it! And use your faith!

This is foundational truth, bedrock truth. When you get this truth under your belt—spiritually speaking—you'll be able to stand against wind, and rain, and flood; Satan and demons, sickness and disease, fear and want.

Part II

FAITH AND BELIEF:
Are they the same?

5

FAITH IS...
a way of walking

We've established that we who are in Christ are to walk according to the Word of God. We *believe* the Word of God, therefore we *DO* the Word of God. The *DOING* of the Word of God is the faith part. In other words, acting on what we believe is faith.

We illustrated how you can believe something and yet never act on it. How you can believe something which is genuinely, historically, scientfically, experientially, true —yet what you believe will never do you as an individual any personal good, unless you act on it. Unless you do something about what you believe.

The doing part is the faith part. That's faith opposed to belief. Both faith and belief, however, have to be in operation to receive the blessing, or the promises, of God.

We pointed out that we in the Body of Christ are to *"walk by faith and not by sight"*. That means we don't walk according to what we see in the physical, tangible universe around us.

All the information and knowledge we receive in the natural realm is received through our five senses— through the eye-gate, the ear-gate, the nose-gate, feeling, etc.

If a man's five senses were destroyed, he'd be helpless. He couldn't learn anything. He couldn't do anything. He couldn't relate to anything because he'd have no sense organs which could respond to stimuli coming to him from the outside world.

What happens is this—many times Christians who are supposed to be walking in the spirit, bring over into the spiritual realm the method they use in the natural realm. That is, they judge things by what they see, and by what they feel. Even though the scripture says we should walk by faith and not by sight—most Christians walk by sight and not by faith.

Our songs are shot through with that idea. For instance, *"Every time I feel the Spirit, moving in my heart, I will pray."* Well, suppose I don't feel the Spirit. Should I not pray? It leaves you with the impression that unless you *feel* something you shouldn't pray.

Many of our songs produce within us a kind of unbelief very difficult to overcome. We don't even realize we're undermining our faith by doing and saying a lot of things which are detrimental to it.

We hear things which appeal to our emotional nature —to the soulish man—and we think it's spiritual because we have a good feeling. But, you see, in the spiritual realm you don't go by feelings. You go by what the Word of God says.

Whatever God says, that's it! That settles it. It's so. No matter how you feel about it. No matter what you see in the natural world. All that is irrelevant, immaterial, and has no bearing at all upon what God says.

I'm healed first of all because the Word says it. Once I start believing and acting upon the Word, the Word will drive out the pain.

But if I wait for the pain to leave to prove to me I'm healed, I'll never get healed. Because Satan is the lord of the sense world. (II Corinthians 4:4) All he'd have to do is put a ring in my nose and lead me around by a *feeling*. And I'd continue to confess the rest of my life that I was sick, simply because I felt pain. I'd be walking by that pain. When you do that you subjugate yourself to Satan because he operates in the sense realm.

God operates in the faith realm. So when I move by what the Word says that pushes out of the way what Satan is bringing to me.

If I should ever get over into the realm of sense knowledge—over into what I feel and sense in my physical body—then I'll be at a disadvantage. I'll be weak in faith, tossed to and fro by every wind which comes along. I'll have no stability. There is no stability in walking by sight, only in walking by faith.

We pointed out from II Kings, Chapter 6, how things exist in two forms. They exist in their spiritual form in the spirit world, where you can't see them and touch them in the natural. They have to be revealed to you by the Holy Spirit and through the Word.

Everything material was first of all spiritual before God made it into the physical. It existed first in the mind of God before it was produced in physical manifestation.

Since everything physical first of all was spiritual, spiritual things are more real than physical things. Just because you can't see a thing, or feel a thing, doesn't mean it doesn't exist. It means you may be moving in a realm where you're not able to perceive it.

For instance, at this very moment, coursing through the air are FM radio waves, AM radio waves, UHF and VHF television pictures in color. If you're not hearing them or seeing them where you are, the reason is you don't have an apparatus tuned in to that frequency. But just because you can't see them, or can't reach out and touch them, or grab a handful of television pictures and throw them up on the wall to be seen, doesn't mean they're not real. It doesn't mean they're not there. And when you get tuned in on the proper apparatus, you can tune in to what is invisible.

Faith is the television set, as it were, which tunes in to the realm of God. Your faith tunes in to that invisible realm. Your Bible is your TV Guide which tells you what's on. Start reading your Guide and find out what programs are on. You'll find it covers everything.

6

FAITH IS...
present tense

HEBREWS 11:1
1 Now faith is the substance of things hoped for,
the evidence of things not seen.

What tense is the following statement? Now faith
is. . . .

It's present tense! It's not, *Yesterday faith was* . . .
nor, *Tomorrow faith is* . . . nor, *Next month faith will be*
. . . it's *NOW FAITH IS.*

NOW FAITH IS THE SUBSTANCE OF THINGS
HOPED FOR, THE EVIDENCE OF THINGS
NOT SEEN.

That is a grammatically correct sentence. And it gives
the definition of what faith is, scripturally speaking.

To illustrate an important truth, I want to drop the
first word of that sentence, the word "now." We'll drop
that word. And we'll capitalize the word "faith" and make
it the first word of the sentence. We want to determine
two things. First of all: Do we still have a grammatically
correct sentence? Then secondly: Do we still have the
definition of faith? If we drop the word "now" will that
change the definition of what's being said here? Let's
read:

FAITH IS THE SUBSTANCE OF THINGS
HOPED FOR, THE EVIDENCE OF THINGS
NOT SEEN.

1 We still have a grammatically correct sentence.
Don't we?

2 We still have the definition of faith. Don't we?

So, whether we put the word "now" in or leave it out
really doesn't change the fact that faith is the substance
of things hoped for and the evidence of things not seen.
If that be true, it almost seems as if the word "now" is
superfluous or unnecessary.

Yet in reality it is quite necessary. For even though you drop the word "now," you still have a grammatically correct sentence, and you still have the definition of faith—but what you wouldn't have would be the *TIME* of faith. So the Holy Spirit puts the "now" in there to let you know that faith is always *NOW*—present tense!

If it's not NOW with you, then it's not faith. That NOW is important. It let's you know faith is always present tense.

Yet I hear people say when I minister to them, "Well, I know that someday . . . in His own good time . . . God is going to heal me."

You might as well sign the death certificate. You're dead now. Forget it. It will never work. Because that is not faith. It's only hope and hope doesn't have any substance. You have to mix faith with it before it will work for you.

If you're waiting for God to meet your present financial need six months from now, forget it! That's not faith. I have to believe that need is met NOW, or it will never work for me.

I can't believe God is going to heal me someday. I'll never get healed. I have to believe I'm healed right NOW before it will work for me. *"NOW FAITH IS. . . ."*

We'll come back to this a little later in the book and show you why this is so. But first, let's examine a couple of other Scriptures which go right along with *"Now faith is. . . ."* It's important for you to see that faith is always right this very second. Always right now. If you're hoping for something to happen someday, then you can tell you're not moving in faith.

MARK 11:24
24 Therefore I say unto you, What things soever ye desire, when ye pray, believe that ye receive them, and ye shall have them.

Jesus is speaking. And He's saying something which is very important. Let's examine it together very carefully. Jesus says. . . .

"THEREFORE I SAY UNTO YOU, WHAT THINGS . . ." There are those things again. Those t-h-i-n-g-s. He didn't say, What dreams . . . or, What thoughts . . . or, What fantasies. He said, *"What things. . . ."*

"THEREFORE I SAY UNTO YOU, WHAT THINGS SOEVER YE DESIRE. . . ." Isn't it interesting that He didn't say, What things soever *GOD* desires for you? He said, "What things soever *YOU* desire." It looks as if the desires are based on what you want. Isn't that what He's saying? It didn't say, Whatever is the will of God . . . or, If it is God's will. It doesn't say that. It says, *"What things soever ye desire. . . ."*

". . . WHEN YE PRAY. . . " All right—*when ye pray* —what tense would that be? That would be NOW, wouldn't it? In other words, *when I pray* is going to be *NOW*. If I pray six months from today, it will be NOW, won't it? It will be *NOW* the very moment *when I pray.*

". . . WHAT THINGS SOEVER YE DESIRE, WHEN YE PRAY, BELIEVE THAT YE RECEIVE THEM. . . ." Believe that you receive them. He didn't say, Feel that you receive them. He didn't say, Understand that you receive them. He said, *"when you pray believe that you receive them and . . ."*

". . . YE SHALL HAVE THEM." "Ye shall have" is a future tense statement. It is future to the "when ye pray." *When I pray* is the same as saying *now faith is.*

To illustrate how carelessly we reason and how easily we can miss it, re-read Mark 11:24 and then I want you to answer something.

MARK 11:24
24 Therefore I say unto you, What things soever ye desire, when ye pray, believe that ye receive them, and ye shall have them.

Answer this question: What is it that you are going to have? What does Jesus say you will have?

The desires? The things? That's where we get hung up—on the desires and the things—and we miss the point.

Here is the point. *"Therefore I say unto you, What things soever ye desire when ye pray, believe that you receive them*—that means right when you pray you have to believe that you receive it—*and you shall have them."* Have what? *THOSE THINGS THAT YOU BELIEVE YOU RECEIVED!* Jesus said you will have what you believe you have already received!

Can you see the difference? He didn't say you would have your desires. He didn't say you would have what you believe. He said you would have what you *BELIEVED YOU'D RECEIVED.* If you don't believe you received anything that's exactly what you're going to get —nothing.

Jesus said you will have what you believed you received. Now if I believe I have already received, then I will say, "Praise God, I believe that I've received." (And here we're getting ready to step on some traditional toes.) And if I believe I have already received it, then I won't pray for it anymore. Because if I pray for it the second time, I'm saying I didn't receive it the first time.

That's how we've been digging a hole for our own faith. We've prayed from sunrise to sunset . . . at every prayer meeting we went to . . . and every Bible class we attended . . . and every evangelist who came to town. We'd go up and have prayer for the same thing over and over and over and over and over again. Every time we did we erased what we'd prayed for the first time. If we believed we had received it, we wouldn't be asking for it again—we wouldn't need to!

Jesus said, *"WHAT THINGS SOEVER YOU DE-SIRE WHEN YOU PRAY. . . ."* He didn't say after you pray. He didn't say when you feel good—or when you felt something—or saw something—or had a vision—or a confirmation—or a revelation. He said, *"When you pray,* simply believe that you have received it."

Believe that you receive it! When? NOW! When you pray!

Then He said, "You shall have. . . ."

You shall have. You shall have. That's future tense. In plain American English—you've got to believe you've

got it before you get it. Do you see that? You have to believe you already have it!

Many try to figure this out in their heads. That's
exactly what trips us up. Faith is not of the head. You
can't get faith in your head. You won't understand any
of the things of God with your head. Because your head
operates by the senses, and the senses immediately tell
you, "I'm not going to say I have something I don't see.
I'd be lying about it."

But you'll save yourself a lot of heartache, a lot of
frustration, a lot of wasted time, if you'll learn this principle—Now faith is.

Jesus said, "When you pray." When you pray would
be NOW. He means the very moment I pray I have to
believe I receive it. I have to believe I receive it right now.
And if I believe that I receive right now I can't ask for it
again. If I ask for it again, I'm saying I didn't get it the
first time.

I JOHN 5:14-15
14 And this is the confidence that we have in
him, that, if we ask any thing according to his
will, he heareth us:
15 And if we know that he hear us, whatsoever
we ask, we know that we have the petitions that
we desired of him.

"Yeah, but Brother Price, that's my problem. I don't
know the will of God."

Well, read the Word. It's in there.

That's the whole problem. Too many are sitting
around on their thumbs instead of reading the Word of
God. *God's will is revealed in His Word.* And it covers
everything you need.

If you don't know the will of God, then we know
what's wrong. You're not in the Word. You may believe
in the Bible and believe that the Bible is the Word of
God, but you won't know God's will until you get in
there and start doing what II Timothy 2:15 says.

*"Study to shew thyself approved unto God, a work-
man that needeth not to be ashamed, rightly dividing the*

word of truth" (II Timothy 2:15). Study. Study. Study— not read—but study. And the very fact that it says to study so you can rightly divide implies that if you don't study you could wrongly divide. Many have wrongly divided. Oh, it's not that they didn't love the Lord, they were just confused and missed the mark.

"And this is the confidence that we have in him, that, if we ask any thing—anything, anything, anything —*according to His will, he heareth us. . . ."* Well, if He heard me, I don't have to shout it 14 times more for Him to hear me—do I? He said He heard me—didn't He? Then it's an insult to ask Him the second time. Because I would be telling Him He didn't hear me the first time, when He tells me He did.

"And if we know (Not if we hope. Not if we feel like it. But if we know.) *that he hear us,* (How do we know that He hears us? He just told us in verse 14 that He did.) *whatsoever we ask,* (Whatsoever would be the same as anything.) *we know* (We don't hope it. We don't feel it. We know.) *that we have the petitions that we desired of him."*

We have them!

Them what? Them petitions.

When do we have them? NOW!

Well if we have them now, we can't ask for them again. Asking for them again is the same as saying we don't have them now and amounts to calling God a liar, because He told us we have them.

"Yes, but I don't see it."

Of course you don't. Faith is the evidence of the thing *not seen*. You have your faith which proves the thing is yours until you can see it. When you can see it, you won't need your faith for it any longer. Until it can be seen, you have your faith as the evidence of the thing not seen. And that faith is based on the Word of God, the Word of the Heavenly Father. He told us that we have it. Does He lie? The Bible says He cannot lie. (Hebrews 6:18) If He told me I have it—I have it! Whether I see it—or whether I don't see it.

FAITH IS...

the title deed

Suppose you walk into a real estate office and say, "I have $30,000 and I would like to buy a piece of property."

The broker shows you photographs of land and buildings. Then he says, "Here is just the one you need."

You say, "That's right. That's the one I want. Here is my $30,000."

The broker writes up a deed of trust.

You haven't even seen the property yet, but you have that deed of trust in your hand. That deed of trust will stand up in the Supreme Court of the United States of America. It will prove to anybody that property belongs to you—all things being equal.

You don't have to see it. Your title deed is the evidence of the thing not seen. One translation of Hebrews 11:1 reads, *"Now faith is the . . . title-deed of the things we hope for, being the proof of things we do not see. . . ."* You don't have to see property in order for it to be yours. If you have a legally recorded title deed you never have to set foot on the property. In fact, you can sell that property to somebody else without ever seeing it. The title deed tells you it's yours.

Faith is the title deed. And that faith is in the Word of God. God doesn't lie. If He says I have it, then I have it. I have it whether I see it or not, because I have a title deed.

Would you fall down on the real estate office floor and cry, "I don't have the property. Maybe I don't really have it. Oh, pray for me that I'll get the property."?

Somebody would walk up and say, "You idiot! You have the title deed right in your hand. What are you crying about?"

We have the title deed—the Bible, God's Word, the Word of Faith. Everything in there—I have. If God says I have it, it's mine. Whether or not I experience it, it's still mine.

Now when I start getting in line with the Word of God and start doing what He says, then I'll experience it. He told me when I pray to believe that I receive it. If I believe that I receive it, that settles it. From then on I just go my way saying, "Praise the Lord. I believe that I have it. I believe I have it. I believe it's mine. I believe I have it. I believe it's mine."

I keep saying that until it manifests. When it physically manifests itself, then I can say, "I have it. Thank you, Father," and that's the end of that transaction. I can go on to something else.

But I won't have it until I *believe that I receive it*. The condition is: I have to believe I have it before I actually get it. That's what faith is. Faith becomes my evidence of the thing not seen—until I see it. Once I see it, I don't need my faith for it any longer.

That's very easy to understand if you'll turn off that gray matter. Just turn your head off. You have to get it in your spirit. This is a spiritual truth.

Jesus said, "... *the words that I speak unto you, they are spirit, and they are life*" (John 6:63). What He meant was, His words are not addressed to man's intellect, but to man's spirit, to the new creature in Christ who lives inside our physical bodies.

When this inner man, the spirit, is grounded in the Word, he will teach the soul, which contains the mind, and the body how to get in line with the Word of God.

What we try to do is get our heads screwed on right. Then we let the head direct the spirit. That's why so many of us are confused, frustrated, sick, poor, and everything else.

If you're going to walk in faith, you'll have to turn your mind off. You can't let your mind dictate to you. You have to let the Word of God dictate to you. You have to fly by the instruments instead of visually.

Flyers take part of their training in what is called a flight simulator. The potential pilot is put into this mock airplane. The hatch is closed over him. He can't visually see outside. He can't see where the trees and mountains and lakes are. All he has in front of him are instruments.

In instrument training he is taught how to fly by these instruments. They tell him where the horizon is, how high or low he is flying, etc.

When they put him in that simulator, they move it around. A motor turns it. As it moves around, he loses his sense of balance and direction. He thinks he's flying straight, or level, when in fact he's flying at an angle. His mind, his head, is telling him he's flying straight when all the time he's flying at an angle. It's hard for the human mind to get away from visually trying to see where the horizon is. But if he watches the instruments, the horizon indicator will tell him he's right on the horizon.

At first our flier makes a lot of mistakes in the simulator. But once he learns how to trust those instruments, he has it made!

As I said earlier, I fly a lot going from one place to another in the teaching ministry, and it never ceases to amaze me how that pilot can fly that big silver bird.

He's up there 40,000 feet in the sky. He comes down over Los Angeles, and it's overcast, smoggy, and hazy. Visibility is only 1,000 feet. You can't see the ground until you're 1,000 feet above it.

Nothing but clouds. I look out the window and see nothing but clouds. But that pilot brings that bird right down on that runway. If he trusted what he saw out the window, he'd crack that plane up. He'd lose his sense of direction. He wouldn't know whether he's flying up or down. He'd look out the window and see nothing but clouds. Sometimes clouds are darker on one side than the other. Sometimes it looks like there's a building or a mountain behind the cloud when there's really nothing there.

But the pilot has learned how to trust his instruments. He follows that radio beam and those meters, gauges, and dials which tell him the altitude and horizon. And he brings it right down every time.

What if he were to look out the window and say, "Now where is the ground? Where is the ground?"

He'd hit the ground before he found out where it was.

God's words are your instruments. If you try to fly by what you see . . . you'll crack up in sickness . . . you'll crack up in poverty . . . you'll crack up in disease . . . you'll crack up in fear . . . and in all the other negatives.

But if you go by what the instruments say! . . .

The instrument says, ". . . . *by whose stripes ye were healed.*" So I don't care what my body tells me. I declare with my mouth, because I believe in my heart that I am healed. And as I continue to say, "I believe that I am healed. I believe that I received it. Thank you, Father. I believe that I am healed," then I bring the plane of my life down perfectly into good health.

Learn to trust your instruments.

7

FAITH IS . . .

in God's eternal now

The reason God tells you, *"NOW FAITH IS. . . ."*—

And the reason Jesus tells you, *". . . WHEN YOU PRAY, believe that you receive. . . ."*—

And the reason I John 5:15 says, *". . . . we know that WE HAVE. . . ."*—

The reason for all this is: When you pray or make your claim to a promise of God, *GOD CANNOT ANSWER YOUR PRAYER EXCEPT RIGHT NOW.*

God doesn't have any tomorrows. God lives in *ONE ETERNAL NOW.* Everything with God is now. There are no yesterdays with God. And there is no tomorrow with God. Everything is right now.

Do you know why that is so? The Bible says God doesn't have a beginning. Don't ask me how that could be so. I don't know. And I don't particularly care. It's a fact. He said it—I believe it—and that's it. God has no beginning, and God doesn't die.

Now if you don't have a beginning, and if you don't die, then seconds, minutes, days, weeks, and years don't mean anything to you. Why? Because you don't have to worry about dying. You'll live forever. Time is inconsequential to you. It's of no consequence whatsoever. It's not important.

God lives in one eternal now. Second Peter 3:8 is often misquoted, but it is a verse which is very important to our subject:

II PETER 3:8

8 But, beloved, be not ignorant of this one thing, that one day is with the Lord as a thousand years, and a thousand years as one day.

Many people misquote that. Some sects do and base their doctrine on it saying, "The Bible says that the Lord says that one day is a thousand years and a thousand years is one day." Then they try to figure out the Day of the Lord saying, "One day equals one thousand years."

That's not what that verse says at all. Read it carefully. It says, *"But, beloved, be not ignorant of this one thing, that one day is with the Lord as a thousand years, and a thousand years as one day."*

You might understand it better if you drop the word "as" and substitute, as we often do today, the word "like." One day is "like" a thousand years and a thousand years is "like" one day to God. Why? Because He doesn't die. He doesn't get any older. God is no older today than He was 50 billion years ago. So to Him one day "is as" a thousand years, and a thousand years "is as" one day. It makes Him no difference. One day could be 50 million years and it wouldn't make any difference. He has no beginning and no ending. Hours and minutes don't mean anything to Him. He lives in one eternal now.

That's why the Scripture says, *"Now faith is. . . ."*

That's why Jesus said, *". . . when you pray, believe that you receive. . . ."*

God can only answer your prayer now. He can only hear you pray now. Stop and think about it. If you pray an hour from now, it's still going to be now. When you pray tomorrow at 12:00 noon, it will still be now when you pray, won't it? When you pray six months from now, it will still be now when you pray. It's always now.

If you can understand this principle and realize God can only answer your prayer right now, then you will understand why the Bible says, "*. . . when you pray, believe that you receive them, and ye shall have them.*"

Since you and I are creatures of time, time means something to us. We have a beginning—we have an ending. Seconds, minutes, days, weeks, months, and years mean a whole lot to us, because we know we're going to die physically someday. We know we had a beginning, we know we were born on such and such a date. And we know we're going to have an ending. Therefore time is important to us.

But to God there is no time. One day with the Lord is as a thousand years. Not, "it is" a thousand years, but it "is as" a thousand years. It's like that to God. Because he has no beginning, and no ending. He only lives in one eternal now.

I know the Bible says in Hebrews 13:8, "*Jesus Christ the same yesterday, and to day, and for ever.*" But that statement is made for our benefit. It's to let us know that yesterday He was the same with us—as He is today with us—as He will be tomorrow with us. The reason for it is He never changes. The Bible says there is not a shadow of turning with God. Why? Because He only lives in one eternal now. Whatever He was yesterday, He is today. Whatever He is today, He will be tomorrow.

So when I pray, I have to believe that I receive my answer right then.

Now in this physical realm there is tangibility, substance. But there is also a spiritual realm out there, a spiritual world. Angels and Satan and demons are out there. Satan and demons are seeking to keep your prayer from being answered, to rob you of your victory, to rob you of your joy, to rob you of your vitality, to rob you of your health. They're out there to trick you and to rob you.

Read the Book of Daniel. You'll find that Daniel had a vision. He wanted to know the interpretation of the vision and he prayed about it. But it was not until 21 days later that the angel Gabriel came to him and said, *"O Daniel, a man greatly beloved . . . from the first day that thou didst set thine heart to understand, and to chasten thyself before thy God, thy words were heard, and I am come for thy words. But the Prince of the Kingdom of Persia withstood me one and twenty days: but, lo, Michael, one of the chief princes, came to help me. . . ."* (Daniel 10:11-13). It was not until Michael, the archangel, came that Gabriel was able to get through.

Here's what happens out there in that spirit world concerning finances, for instance.

Do you think God drops money out of the sky? It's amazing how we can think things without having any scriptural basis for them. I used to think—in my mind I had the idea—that if I needed money, God would just reach over the balcony of heaven and say, "Hey, Fred," and drop down $10.00.

God can't do that. If he did that, He'd be a counterfeiter. All the money is already in circulation. Anybody who introduces additional money into the economy of the United States of America is considered a counterfeiter. So the money is already here.

All right, God knows where it all is. And God can move on the hearts of men.

And not only that, but there is sometimes money which has been lost by men, and the angels know where it is. The New Testament talks about angels being ministering spirits, sent forth to minister for us who are the heirs of salvation. (Hebrews 1:14) And it doesn't say to minister "to" them—it says to minister "for" them. In other words, "on their behalf." When we pray, the angels are the ones who bring that money to us. When I say they bring it, it's through men—money is going to come through some human hand—but angels are behind it, moving in that spirit realm, channeling that money to God's people when they pray and believe and stand steadfast in it.

In the meantime, Satan's angels, his demons, are trying to keep the angels of God from getting to you with the answer. The thing that turns the tide is your faith. Your standing on the claim you have made and continuing to thank the Lord that you believe you have received it is what turns the tide for the angels of God. Then they can get through with the answer.

Now, since we are creatures of time, it appears to us there is a time element—a day, a week, a month, a year—before we get the answer. But as far as God is concerned, the moment you prayed it, He answered it then. Now, based upon your standing in faith and based upon your acting on His Word, the thing you've prayed for will come into physical manifestation.

As you use your faith and it grows stronger, the time factor between the time you pray and the time the manifestation comes grows shorter and shorter. For as you stand in faith and become more mature, and your faith is exercised in a more deliberate and definite manner, Satan and demons will know they can't lord it over you and that you're going to stand on the Word of God.

8

FAITH IS ...

a confession

When I've claimed—whatever it is I've claimed—then I must confess that I believe I have it.

Many times people say, "Well, I'm not going to say I'm healed when I still hurt. And if somebody asks me how I feel, and I feel terrible, I can't tell them that I feel good. I'd be lying, wouldn't I?"

Certainly. You would be.

But I want you to notice something. In Mark 11:24, Jesus said, *"Therefore I say unto you, What things soever ye desire, when ye pray, BELIEVE that ye receive them. . . ."* He didn't say, *FEEL* like it. He said, *BELIEVE* it.

Take healing for instance. If I've claimed my healing for a condition, then I say, "Lord, I believe according to your Word, according to Matthew 8:17, which says, *'. . . Himself took our infirmities, and bare our sickness'*, and according to I Peter 2:24, which says, *'. . . by whose stripes ye were healed.'* By His stripes I was healed. If I was, then I am. ('I am' is present tense.) According to your Word, I believe I am healed."

In the physical, I may have no change whatsoever. I may even have a change for the worse. Because many times, especially in the areas of healing, the moment you get into this realm and start moving in faith, Satan will really put the screws on you. For he is the author of sickness and disease. He is the agent that brings sickness and disease to you.

(Now if you're living in open sin and rebellion against the will of God, you open the door for Satan to put sickness and disease on you. You can't live in known sin and expect to walk in good health. You can't shack up with somebody and live as husband and wife without being married and think you're going to get faith to work for you. That nullifies it. If there's any other thing you know you're not doing right, then you can't expect faith to work in that kind of atmosphere. We're talking about the individual who loves the Lord and is desirous to walk in the center of His perfect will, who is doing everything he knows how to do to live right.)

So, I make my claim and say, "Father, I believe that I receive my healing. I believe that I am healed."

Satan, the author of sickness and disease, works in the sense realm. So he'll keep hitting my body with the pain. Then he'll shoot a thought into my mind and say, "You're sick."

That's how Satan gets an advantage over you. He throws a dart of sickness or disease to your body. Immediately upon the dart's hitting your body you feel pain. Immediately Satan throws another dart to your mind with the suggestion, "Apparently you're coming down with the flu."

Then you pick it up. You hear people do it all the time, "I think I'm taking a cold." "I think I'm going to be sick." "My heart—there must be something wrong with my heart."

You may not realize it, but *WHAT YOU SAY IS WHAT YOU GET.*

Proverbs 18:21 says, *"Death and life are in the power of the tongue. . . ."* That's pretty strong. The power of life and death is in the tongue.

And Proverbs 6:2 says, *"Thou art snared with the words of thy mouth, thou art taken with the words of thy mouth."* A snare is a trap. You are trapped by the words of your mouth. Therefore you have to watch what you say. You have to learn how to say only what God's Word says. You can't say what you feel.

Somebody says, "Yeah, but if I do that I'm lying."

No, you're not.

By faith I believe that I receive my healing. This is a faith matter.

(Keep in mind that receiving by your faith is one thing, and receiving through *gifts of healings* or *working of miracles* [I Corinthians 12] is another thing entirely. *Gifts of healings or working of miracles* are not based on the recipient's faith at all, but upon the sovereign grace work of the Holy Spirit. Faith is not involved at all when *gifts of the Holy Spirit* operate as far as the person who receives the healing or the miracle is concerned.)

In the realm of faith where I-am-believing-and-acting-upon-the-Word-of-God-for-myself, 99 and 9/10 percent of the time the physical manifestation of the healing will be a process. There will be a time element. It may be a minute, a day, an hour, a week. But the physical manifestation will come if you dare to believe it and hold fast to your confession. As you continue to use your faith and grow in it, the interim period between the time you make a claim for healing—or whatever—until the time it physically manifests will become shorter and shorter.

I'll give you a personal illustration.

When I was junior high school age, I contracted a growth about the size of a green pea in my chest cavity. It grew and developed. After I became a man and was married, this thing had grown to the size of a silver dollar. It was just under the skin. I could feel it pressing against the mammary gland just beneath the nipple in the left side of my chest. It was excruciatingly hurtful.

At that time I didn't know anything about healing. I didn't know that God would heal. I'd never been taught that. The churches I'd been to didn't say anything about healing. In fact, what little they did say about it was that it all went out with the early church. They said we didn't have it anymore. They said God gave us doctors instead of miracles. And I believed it.

(Divine healing is not in opposition to medical science. Thank God for doctors. It's just that God has a better way than getting your leg cut off.)

The pain was terrible, so I went to a surgeon.

The surgeon said, "Yes, Mr. Price, you have a tumor."

I had surgery. The operation was a success. It was benign.

But the doctor said, "There is only one thing we want to warn you about. With this particular kind of tumor, vestiges of it could remain in the blood stream and there is a possibility it could float over into the other side of your chest cavity and begin to develop."

At that time there was nothing wrong with the right side of my chest. But, as time went on, I noticed a little growth under the skin about the size of a green pea as I was showering one day. I didn't pay any attention to it. But as time went on it grew to the size of a dime, then to the size of a quarter, and then it was back to that silver dollar size, and the pain was almost unbelievable. I could hardly bear to have my shirt lie against it. I couldn't lie down on my right side because it hurt so badly. It hurt like somebody would take an ice pick and stick you in the eye.

But now, at this point in my life, I knew what the Word said! I'd found out that God Himself, my Heavenly Father said, " . . . *I am the Lord that healeth thee*" (Exodus 15:26). (Remember how when God sent Moses down to Pharaoh and Moses said, "Who shall I say sent me." And God said, "Tell them I AM THAT I AM has sent you." (See Exodus 3:13-14.) I AM is present tense. Nowhere in the Bible do you ever find where God said, I was. And you'll never find Him saying, I will be. He always says, I AM. Jesus took up the same thing and during His ministry He always said, "I am the bread of life." Not, I'm going to be. He said, "I am the light of the world." Not, I'm trying to be. He said, "I AM." That's always present tense. Always NOW.)

And at this point in my life I knew that God said, ". . . *Himself took our infirmities, and bare our sicknesses*" (Matthew 8:17).

And I'd found out I Peter 2:24 says, ". . . *by whose stripes ye were healed.*" So I said, "Bless God, if I were —(were is past tense)—then I was. If I was—then I am!

In January of 1972 I took my Bible. I stood up in my room. And I said, "Father, I want to call you into record. Holy Ghost, I call you into record. Jesus, I call you into record as a witness. Angels of heaven, I call you into record. Satan and all his demons, I call you into record this day that I take my stand on the Word of the Living God.

"I declare with my mouth, according to Matthew 8:17, which says, '. . . *Himself took our infirmities, and bare our sicknesses.*' If he took mine and bore mine, then I don't have to take them and bear them. And according to I Peter 2:24, which says, '. . . *by whose stripes ye were healed.*' If I was, then I am.

"And then, Mark 11:24 says, '. . . *What things soever ye desire, . . .*' I desire to be well. '. . . *when ye pray, . . .*' I am praying now. '. . . *believe that ye receive them, . . .*' I now believe that I receive healing for this tumor condition. '. . . *and ye shall have them.*' I declare with my mouth that I believe that I receive, therefore I shall have it.

"I thank you for it, Father. That settles it. I believe that I am now healed."

That was January, 1972. January, February, March came—three months later. The growth grew larger and the pain grew worse. There was no physical change for the better whatsoever. In fact, the physical change went for the worse.

During that time I never said I was healed. Jesus never said to say that you have the thing. He said to say that you believe you have it. That's the difference. And what I believe is based on what He told me, so I can't be lying about it.

We looked at the account of the angels at Dothan. The angels were already there. Gehazi just couldn't see them. When God by His Spirit gave him the manifestation of the discerning of spirits, Gehazi saw into the spirit world. And he saw horses and chariots of fire. But they were already there. He just couldn't see them in the natural.

All right, so if Jesus tells me to *believe that I receive when I pray,* then whatever I *believe that I receive* must already be in existence. It is my faith which brings them into manifestation. So I said, "Father, I thank you, I believe that I am healed."

I couldn't have used my body as evidence I was healed, because I still had the tumor. In the natural the tumor was still in my body. In fact, it had grown larger and it hurt worse. I never said I was healed. I never said I didn't hurt. If I had said that I didn't hurt, I would have been lying. I never talked about anything in the natural. I ignored it. *All I talked about was what I believed.*

I would never confess what I felt. I would never confess what I saw. I would only confess with my mouth what I believed, and I couldn't be lying because Jesus told me to believe it. He told me when I prayed to believe that I received it and then I'd have it. So all I did was say, "I believe that I am healed." And I did. I believed it because He told me. I didn't believe it because I felt like it—because I didn't feel like it.

I never went around saying I didn't hurt when in fact I did hurt. If you do that you're getting over into the realm of Christian Science and the mind science religions. You're saying the thing doesn't exist. We're not saying sickness and disease don't exist. I've never said the tumor wasn't a reality. I never said it wasn't there. I never said the thing wasn't hurting. I didn't say anything about it at all. I ignored it. I only talked about what I believed.

And I said, "I believe that I am well. I believe that I am healed." And I did believe because the Word of the Lord said to believe that I receive and I'd have it. Bless God, I believed that I received it and I was prepared to stand there ten million years if it took that long for the physical evidence to come.

January, February, March, April, May, June—six months later. And the growth grew larger, and the pain grew worse.

Satan was screaming in my ear, "You are a fool, Fred Price. You're not healed. Reach over there and touch it. Feel it."

(See how all of that—touch, feel—is in the sense realm. If Satan can get you over in the sense realm, he'll whip you. But if you keep him in the faith realm, you'll destroy him. You'll put him under your feet.)

I told him, "Devil, I didn't say that I was healed because I looked like it. I didn't tell you that I was healed because I felt like it. I said that I believe that I've received my healing. I received it in January. I received it then based on the Word of God. And I believe that I am healed now. If you say I'm not, you're a liar. And you are one anyway, Jesus said you were the father of it. If you don't believe I'm healed, you're going to have to argue with God, because He wrote it and I'm doing what He told me. I believe that I am healed."

In my body I didn't feel healed. But I wouldn't confess what my body said. Often I felt bad and somebody would ask, "I heard you received your healing. How do you feel?"

(That's the normal, natural transition of questions. "I heard that you were healed—how do you feel?" See? And that's the door that opens up for Satan to walk right in and defeat you.)

This is what I learned to do—and this is what you'll have to learn to do. If somebody asked me, "Fred, how do you feel now?", I would say, "Well, praise God, according to the Word of God, II Corinthians, Chapter 5, verse 7, '. . . *we walk by faith and not by sight.*' And because the Word of God tells me in Mark 11:24 that what things soever I desire when I pray to believe that I receive them and I shall have them—I have already prayed and I believe that I have received my healing. And I'm walking by faith and not by sight, so I'm doing fine. How about you?"

See? I didn't lie. I just didn't give any consideration to the natural. I dealt only with the spiritual. Only with what I believe. If I had said with my mouth, "I am not in pain," I would have been lying. If I had said with my mouth, "There isn't any growth there," I would have been lying. I didn't say that. I said only what I believed.

I said, "I believe that I am healed." And I did. Because the Word of God told me.

July, August, September—nine months later. Every day in my prayer time I said, "Lord, I thank you. I believe that I am healed." I never said I was. He said that I was. I believed what He said, so I believe that I am. By faith I believe that I am healed.

Because my faith is based on the Word of God and He said that by His stripes I was healed, I have evidence. Faith is my evidence, according to Hebrews 11:1. I could not look to my body. My body had no evidence that I was healed. My body had evidence that I was sick. But I didn't look at my body. I looked only to the Word of God.

The Word of God said that with His stripes I was healed. So that's what I kept saying, because that's what I was believing.

October, November. Over 300 days I kept saying every day, "Lord, I thank you. I believe I am healed. I believe I'm healed."

I didn't feel like it. The growth continued to grow larger and the pain grew worse. All that time, I never did confess what I felt and I never did confess what I saw, I confessed only what I believed. I had the Bible as my evidence, the Word of God. Until you can prove with your body that you're healed, you have to rely on God's Word in faith. Once you have the physical manifestation in your physical body, then you can say, "I am healed. Examine my body and see." Until your physical body shows the signs of the healing, then you can say, "I believe I'm healed. Look at the Word of God. It proves it." Because God said it, nobody will argue.

The latter part of November—the first part of December—I don't know when it was. I was taking a shower and soaping up with the wash cloth. As I washed on my right side, I didn't feel that usual pain. I dropped that cloth and grabbed my chest. The thing had disappeared! I don't even know when it left and could care less. It was gone then, and it's gone now. It disappeared. Faith drove it out.

Now I was a baby in faith in 1972, just learning about it. Therefore when I heard and read these truths, I accepted them immediately with my intellect, my mind. But the truth hadn't really sunk down into the inner man, the spirit. I was believing it with my mind. I kept saying it because I believed it. If you keep doing that, you'll school yourself into faith. By continuing to say it because you believe it—because you want to believe it—it will come to pass. What happened was it finally got down into my spirit.

But because you walk in faith and because you have been healed doesn't mean Satan won't try to put something else on you. He tries to attack with one thing after the other. But none of it ever gets through to me. I never accept any of it. I never sign for any of the packages, because they don't have my name on them.

A process server goes out with a subpoena. He has to put that subpoena in my hand before it's legal and binding. Once I take it, the court can enforce it.

Satan comes out with the symptom—flu, cold, heart trouble, whatever. By saying it, "Well, I think I'm going to be sick," you accept the subpoena of sickness in your hand. Now Satan and demons can jump in your chest and enforce it and make it stick in your physical body."

When they come to me with the sickness, I say, "That's not mine. You can't stop here at my house. Take that somewhere else. It's not mine. Do you know why? Because with His stripes I was healed. If I was—I am. Therefore I can't be sick." And he just walks on by.

Certainly I'm attacked. Satan hates these truths. He hates me because I deliver them. But don't think I'm anybody special. He hates you too. He hates your guts. And he'll kill you if he gets the chance.

He tries to put something on me and then he tells me, "Isn't that something. You're going to talk about divine healing and look at you. You have this—and you have that."

I say, "I don't have anything, devil, but divine health. That's all I have. That's your confession, not mine. I believe I am well."

I've stood and ministered when my physical body was in pain. But you see, I am not healed because I feel like I'm healed. I am healed because the Word of God declares that it is so.

Divine healing is not true because people get healed. Divine healing is true *BECAUSE GOD SAID IT*. If nobody in the world was ever healed, it would not invalidate divine healing.

You say, "I don't understand that."

It's very simple. Suppose nobody ever believed that Jesus was the Son of God and nobody ever accepted Him as Saviour. How many people would get saved? None! But would that mean Jesus didn't die at Calvary? Whether folks get saved or not doesn't have a thing to do with Jesus dying and providing salvation. Whether or not you get saved does not make salvation true.

All right, because you get healed or don't get healed doesn't make divine healing true. Divine healing is true because the Word of God declares it's true. And because it is true, you can be healed.

I use healing as an example because the Lord uses me in a ministry along the lines of faith and healing. But the principle of praying and believing that you receive works the same in every area of our lives.

Jesus told me when I pray to believe that I receive it. It doesn't matter whether it's money, finances, a new job, a new home, or whatever—the principle works the same. I have to believe that I receive it when I pray.

Again, that's assuming I'm living in line with the Word of God. You see, living by faith doesn't mean you quit your job, go out in the park, get some bread from somewhere, and sit out there feeding the birds, expecting God to send the ravens to feed you.

To live by faith doesn't mean you give up your job. It means that you don't look to the job as your source of supply. You look to God as your source—and to your job as only one of many channels by which God provides your needs. The Scripture says that those who wouldn't work shouldn't eat. (II Thessalonians 3:10) So living by faith doesn't mean you go out on the street and say, "I'm just going to trust the Lord." That's presumption—not faith.

IN SUMMATION: Parts I and II

We see that faith and belief are not the same. I can believe all day long and receive nothing. Even though what I believe may be true, it will not affect me in a personal way until I start acting on what I believe. We recall our example of the starving man who said he believed that eating the food would keep him from starving to death. Yet he died with food in plain sight. Why? Simply because he did not eat the food. He did not act on what he believed.

Part III

9

FAITH IS...
acting on the Word

Faith is acting on the Word. No matter how much you talk about how you believe the Bible is the Word of God—No matter how much you may mouth off about how you believe the Bible from Genesis to Revelation—No matter how much you sing the praises of the Bible as the greatest story ever told—No matter how often you repeat the oft quoted phrase "the Bible is the world's best seller" —You can say all that, and talk about all that—but if you don't ACT on what the Bible says, then the promises of the Bible and all declared therein will never do you any personal good in your personal everyday existence.

It is not enough to believe the Bible is true. It is not enough to believe the Bible is the Word of God. It is not enough to believe that what is recorded on the pages of the Bible is truly inspired of God. It will not do you any good personally in your everyday life until you begin to ACT on that Word. Faith is acting on the Word of God.

The more I travel and minister along the lines of faith, the more I am made aware that people do not really know what faith is. They don't know how to appropriate the promises of God. They don't know how to move the hand of God. Oh, they know how to sing and shout, how to make noise and clap their hands and lift them. But they don't know how to move the hand of God. They don't know how to exercise faith. They do not understand it.

They haven't learned how to ACT on the Word. They quote scriptures. They say, "Oh, I know that's in the

Bible. I know the Bible says that." It won't do you any good to KNOW it's in there—you have to learn how to ACT on it. Faith is ACTING!

Faith is an action. You have to act on what you believe. You say you believe the Bible, then DO what the Bible says. You say you believe the Word of God, then DO the Word of God—ACT on it.

I was reading recently in the Gospel of Luke. I'd read Luke 21 times before, but these scriptures jumped out at me. That's why the Bible says to study to show yourself approved. (II Timothy 2:15)

Some people read it once and figure, "I know what the Bible says. I read the Bible."

Reading it once, they don't even know where a period is. They read it once and think they know it. They read the Bible like you'd read the newspaper, like you'd read the sports section. And they think they know it. They don't know squatdoodlely about the Bible. If they did, they'd be DOING it. Not talking about it—but DOING it.

"Oh, I know the Bible says this. And I know the Bible says that."

DO IT then. DO IT. If you don't do it, you don't know it. You may think you know it, but if you knew it, you'd do it.

If somebody gave you a bottle of poison and said, "Drink this," but right on the label it said, "POISON," and you said, "Oh, I know this is poison," would you drink it? No! You wouldn't DO IT, would you?

That works in reverse. If you know what TO DO, you're supposed TO DO IT. If you're not doing it, you don't really believe it. If that label had the skull and crossbones on it and said POISON, and you said, "Hmmm, I don't think that's really poison," and you drank it down, it would kill you just the same.

As I said, though I'd read the Gospel of Luke 21 times before, the Spirit of God brought this scripture to my attention in a new and living way. It jumped off the page at me. I saw it in a new light. Not that the truth changed, but there was an amplification of truth. I saw the truth in a new way and I want to share it with you.

LUKE 5:4-7

4 Now when he (Jesus) had left speaking, he said unto Simon, Launch out into the deep, and let down your nets for a draught.

5 And Simon answering said unto him, Master, we have toiled all the night, and have taken nothing: nevertheless at thy word I will let down the net.

6 And when they had this done, they enclosed a great multitude of fishes: and their net brake.

7 And they beckoned unto their partners, which were in the other ship, that they should come and help them. And they came, and filled both the ships, so that they began to sink.

Here's where we miss it. We miss God because we look at things in the natural. We're dominated by sense-knowledge—what we can see, what we can feel, what we can taste, what we can touch, what we can hear. And we are not governed by, or operating by, what the Word of God declares.

Peter could have said, "Lord, we've fished all night long. You're a carpenter. You just came out of Nazareth from a carpenter's shop. We've been out here on the lake fishing for years. This is our job. This is our livelihood. This is what we do for a living. If anybody knows where the fish are, and when to fish, and how to catch them, we know it. You're going to tell us how to fish and you're a carpenter?"

That's how we do God. "What does God know about my problems. Has He ever had a nagging husband or a nagging wife? What does He know about this situation. Has He ever had kids that are driving Him up the wall? What does God know about this? Has He ever suffered? Has He ever been sick? What does God know? He's telling me to believe I'm healed and I know I'm not. I still have the pain."

But instead, Peter said, "We've toiled all night. We've fished all night, and have caught nothing." I know what

Peter was talking about. I've done that myself—fished a whole cotton-pickin' day and didn't even get a nibble.

But then Peter said, ". . . *nevertheless at thy word I will let down the net.*" There's the secret of faith! There it is right there—at thy Word. At THY WORD! Not at my experience. Not at what I see. Not at what we have already done and failed in. But *AT YOUR WORD,* I'll let down the net.

Many times God in His Word tells us to do things which in the natural seem ridiculous. They seem impossible. They defy logic. Yet God says to do it.

You look at that thing in the context of the natural and you say, "Man, that's impossible. How can I do that? How can you love somebody when they just spit on you? How can you love them when they just lied about you? He said, 'Love your enemies.' Man, that's crazy. He ain't never had nobody spit on Him like that. Man, it's hard to take when somebody tells all kinds of lies about you. What does God know about that? He tells me to love them anyhow. That ain't gonna work. I'll tell you what I'm gonna do, an eye for an eye and a tooth for a tooth. That's what I'm gonna do. Love 'em? Turn the other cheek? That's for fools."

Is it? "We've toiled all night, and have taken nothing—nevertheless *AT THY WORD* I'll let down the net."

Here was a situation where it seemed absolutely impossible anything could come of it. These men were experienced fishermen. They did this every day of their lives. It was their job. They knew where the schools of fish were, when the fish were running, when the tide was up, when the winds were blowing, when to put the nets down. And they had toiled all night and had taken nothing.

Here comes Jesus, a carpenter, and says, "Let down your nets for a draught."

Peter says, "We've toiled all night, and have taken nothing, nevertheless at thy Word—just because you said it—for no other reason—I have no other evidence to go on—but you said it—I'll let down the net."

What happened?

"And when they had this done, they enclosed a great multitude of fishes: and their net brake." All night they couldn't catch a thing. Jesus said, "Drop your net right there," and the net began to break. They brought another boat and both boats were sinking because they had so many fish.

How did it all come about? By *ACTING* on the Word of God.

Do *YOU* do that? Do you *ACT* on God's Word?

It's simply abandoning all of your philosophical reasonings, abandoning all of your logical mental processes, and merely exercising faith in doing what His word says.

Jesus said, "Let down your nets."

Peter said, "We've toiled all night and taken nothing, *NEVERTHELESS AT THY WORD. . . .*"

FAITH IN ACTION ...

at Jericho

JOSHUA 6:1-2

1 Now Jericho was straitly shut up because of the children of Israel: none went out, and none came in.

2 And the LORD said unto Joshua, See, I have given into thine hand Jericho, and the king thereof, and the mighty men of valour.

This is the way God operates. God operates and speaks as though the thing had already happened, even though in the natural it hasn't happened yet. Joshua and the children of Israel were outside the walls of Jericho. The city was shut up. The gates were locked. The men of Jericho were on the battlements ready for battle because they were afraid of Israel. They had heard how God brought them through the wilderness and the Red Sea, and they were scared to death of these people of God.

God said to Israel before they ever went into the city, *"I HAVE GIVEN INTO THINE HAND. . . ."* Not, I'm going to give it to you. I have given it to you. That's past tense, brother. I have means it's already done. Yet they're standing outside the walls!

God says, "I have already supplied your needs," and you're whining and crying and belly-aching because you can't pay the rent. That's because you don't believe the Word.

"Oh yes, I believe the Bible from Genesis to Revelation."

Yes, but you're not ACTING on it. You're repudiating what you believe about the Bible when you say, "I can't pay my rent. I don't have money to do this. I don't have money to do that." You're saying you don't have it when God says your needs are met.

"Yes, but that don't make sense."

You're right. It doesn't. It's not sense. It's *faith*. Faith is not sense, and sense is not faith. Dogs are not cats, and cats are not dogs. Dogs are dogs, and cats are cats. Faith is faith, and sense is sense. It's just that simple.

God said, "I have given it to you." For you see the Bible says that God calleth those things which be not as though they were. (Romans 4:17) That's what faith does.

"That don't make sense."

You're right. It doesn't. But follow on.

JOSHUA 6:3-4

3 And ye shall compass the city, all ye men of war, and go round about the city once. Thus shalt thou do six days.

4 And seven priests shall bear before the ark seven trumpets of rams' horns: and the seventh day we shall compass the city seven times, and the priests shall blow with the trumpets.

"Those are the most ridiculous instructions I ever heard anybody give anybody else. Isn't that the dumbest thing you ever heard of—everyday go around the walls of this city one time, blow some trumpets, then go back to camp for six days, then on the seventh day walk around

the walls seven times and blow on the trumpets? Man,
that doesn't make sense."

You're right. It doesn't. But follow on.

JOSHUA 6:5a

5 And it shall come to pass, that when they make
a long blast with the ram's horn, and when ye
hear the sound of the trumpet, all the people
shall shout with a great shout; . . .

"Man, this is really ridiculous. Blowing the horns was
bad enough, but now He wants us to shout."

We've toiled all night and taken nothing, nevertheless
at thy Word we'll let down the net.

You say you believe the Bible—then you'll do it. You
say you believe the Word—then do it. If you don't do it,
you don't believe it. And if you don't do it, you won't get
the benefits and results of it. It's just that simple.

JOSHUA 6:5b

5 . . . and the wall of the city shall fall down
flat, and the people shall ascend up every man
straight before him.

"These are the most ridiculous instructions I've ever
heard of. Illogical. Nonsensical. Stupid. Dumb. Unreasonable. And any other negative you can think of."

But God said, "I have given it to you."

You see, we miss God because we try to put it through
the computer of the little pea which sits between our
shoulder blades. We try to figure it out in our head when
all God expects us to do is to act on His Word. Then the
understanding comes. We want to understand first, and
then we'll do it. But that's not faith. It's not until you act
in faith that your understanding will really be enlighten-
ed as it ought to be. In matters of faith and matters of the
spirit understanding comes after action.

In the natural we want to know everything and then
do it. But even in the natural we exercise the same principle of faith every day of our lives and never give it a
question. Yet when it comes to the things of God, who
created the universe and sustains the action of the stars,
we want to question Him about the authenticity of what

He tells us to do. Every day we do a thousand and one things not knowing how, or why, or having rhyme or reason of how the thing works. We just accept it.

I use a tape recorder almost every day. I have yet to figure out how in the world my voice gets on a piece of tape. Maybe you understand it, but I don't. I cannot understand how I can talk into a little microphone, and it runs through a wire, is put on a little piece of flimsy plastic tape, and I can take that tape and play it back on a machine and hear my voice again saying the very same thing. I don't understand that. But I just put that tape on there and play it. It doesn't make me any difference whether I understand it or not. It works! What do I care if I know how a tape recorder works. It works and I get the results. Isn't that what you want?

Do you know how television works? Do you know how a little box in your house picks a picture up out of the sky? In color? Suppose you had to understand that before you could turn on your set. None of us would ever look at television, would we?

The other day I talked to a man up in Seattle, Washington. He's up in Seattle, and I'm down in Los Angeles. And he's talking to me just like he was in the next room. Just by dialing some numbers—blam!—there he was! I don't understand how that works. How my voice can travel all those miles. But I don't have to understand to dial a number and talk to the man and get the information I want. I don't have to know that, do I?

Yet when it comes to the things of God, we want a blueprint, a schematic diagram. We want to submit it to a computer, have it analyzed, spectrographed, and the whole bit, before we're ready to act.

We've toiled all night and have taken nothing, nevertheless at thy Word.

In the natural, the instructions God gave Israel were ridiculous.

"I mean, what a way to go. Why don't you just walk right on up to the door, knock it down, and let us go on in and get the thing on? Why waste seven days?"

Yes, but that's God's way.

Who are you, speck of dust, to say to God, "Why?" Who are you, insignificant worm, to question God?

That's like Job running off at the mouth about what shouldn't have happened—his mother and father shouldn't have come together and all that kind of junk. God finally got fed up and just said, "Now listen. Stand up here and shut your mouth, gird yourself up, and answer these questions. Where were you when I laid the foundation of the world? Answer me if you can. Where were you when the sons of God shouted for joy and the morning stars sang together?"

Where were you, Big Mouth? And you're going to tell God how to do it?

See how silly that is. We're going to tell God.

Who are you?

JOSHUA 6:6-11

6 And Joshua the son of Nun called the priests, and said unto them, Take up the ark of the covenant, and let seven priests bear seven trumpets of rams' horns before the ark of the LORD.

7 And he said unto the people, Pass on, and compass the city, and let him that is armed pass on before the ark of the LORD.

8 And it came to pass, when Joshua had spoken unto the people, that the seven priests bearing the seven trumpets of rams' horns passed on before the LORD, and blew with the trumpets: and the ark of the covenant of the LORD followed them.

9 And the armed men went before the priests that blew with the trumphets, and the rereward came after the ark, the priests going on, and blowing with the trumpets.

10 And Joshua had commanded the people, saying, Ye shall not shout, nor make any noise with your voice neither shall any word proceed out of your mouth, until the day I bid you shout; then shall ye shout.

11 So the ark of the LORD compassed the city, going about it once: and they came into the camp, and lodged in the camp.

I can imagine the people of Jericho looking out over the walls saying, "That's the dumbest bunch of people we've ever seen. What are they doing down there? Look at those idiots. They walked around the wall, blew the trumpets, and then went back to their camp. Can you understand that? I don't understand what they're doing."

I can imagine the news media out there with television cameras trying to figure out what in the world is going on. The TV reporter covering the story would report, "They come up to the walls. They march around them in battle array. Their priests walk around the wall and blow their trumpets. Then they go back to their camp." I can imagine the news analysts trying to figure it all out.

We've toiled all night and caught nothing, nevertheless at thy Word.

JOSHUA 6:12-16; 20

12 And Joshua rose early in the morning, and the priests took up the ark of the LORD,

13 And seven priests bearing seven trumpets of rams' horns before the ark of the LORD went on continually, and blew with the trumpets: and the armed men went before them; but the rereward came after the ark of the LORD, the priests going on, and blowing with the trumpets.

14 And the second day they compassed the city once, and returned into the camp: so they did six days.

15 And it came to pass on the seventh day, that they rose early about the dawning of the day, and compassed the city after the same manner seven times: only on that day they compassed the city seven times.

16 And it came to pass at the seventh time, when the priests blew with the trumpets, Joshua said

unto the people, Shout; for the LORD hath given you the city . . .

20 So the people shouted when the priests blew with the trumpets: and it came to pass, when the people heard the sound of the trumpet, and the people shouted with a great shout, that the wall fell down flat, so that the people went up into the city, every man straight before him, and they took the city.

It may not have fit logic. It may not have been reasonable. But it worked! They took the city!

"Yes, but why did God go through all that?"

I don't know. But what difference does it make? They took the city!

If somebody wants to give you a million dollars are you going to squabble about whether you get it in tens or twenties? Man, give me the million dollars. I'll take it in pennies. And I'll have a glorious time counting those pennies.

What difference does it make whether they got the city in one day or seven? The point is when they were obedient to the Word of God—when they acted—when they did the Word—results came! And not until then!

We've toiled all night and have taken nothing, nevertheless AT THY WORD.

What is the Word of God saying to us? Many things! Are we DOING them?

The Bible says, *"Be careful* (anxious) *for nothing . . . ."* (Philippians 4:6). Yet when I minister people come up to me who are nervous, afraid, and fearful. It's easy to show them the problem. They're not ACTING on the Word.

"Oh, I believe it from Genesis to Revelation."

But they're not doing it. And because they don't do it, it doesn't work on their behalf. If you'll believe that Word and do it, you'll never be afraid of anything. Brother they can bring Rodan through the door and it won't make any difference—even King Kong and all his boys.

"Yes, I believe the Bible."

Well, the Bible tells you to be anxious for nothing. The Amplified translation of Philippians 4:6 reads, *"Do not fret or have any anxiety about anything. . . ."* It means we're not to take any care or fret over anything.

Yet how many fret over bills, over money, over husbands or wives, over jobs, etc., while they say they believe the Word. That's why it doesn't work for them. It won't work until you do what that Word says.

FAITH IN ACTION . . .

in everyday affairs

The scriptural illustrations I'm giving are to show you what the Word of God is teaching us—the secret of faith. *FAITH is ACTING ON THE WORD*—not on your emotions, not on your feelings, not on some philosophical reasonings, not on theological concepts, but it's *acting* on God's Word.

That Word works! Hallelujah, it works! I've seen it over and over and over and over again, miracle after miracle, healing after healing, deliverance after deliverance. That Word works when you DO what it says, even while your mind is shouting and screaming at you that it's illogical, that it will not work, that it's foolishness, that you're going to be made a fool of.

At thy Word—that's the secret. At thy Word, *"Be careful for nothing. . . ."*

"But I have financial problems."

The only thing I can tell you is what I tell myself. The Bible says in Philippians 4:19, *"But my God shall supply all your need according to his riches in glory by Christ Jesus."*

If you believe that Word, then do that Word. If you believe your needs are met you'll stop crying and worrying about them. You'll leave it in God's hands.

We say we believe the Word, then we go to the loan company and borrow the money to pay the bill. You can do that without God. An atheist can do that. All you have to do is have pretty good credit.

"Yes, I believe the Bible."

Stop worrying then.

"Oh, Pastor, I'd like for you to pray for me. I'm afraid. I have fear."

In answer to that I say, "Here's what I do. I believe what the Bible says. The Bible says that I have not been given the spirit of fear, but of power, and of love, and of a sound mind. (II Timothy 1:7) So I refuse to be afraid."

I used to be afraid of a lot of things. Yes, as a Christian. As a preacher. Afraid of airplanes. I wouldn't go in an airplane. You couldn't put me in an airplane at gun point. You couldn't handcuff me—they didn't have gorillas big enough to get me on board a plane. You talk about putting up a scuffle—man, I would have fought like a tiger.

"What do you mean, get me on an airplane?" I'd say. "You ain't getting me up in no airplane. That crazy pilot might have a heart attack. It just might be the Lord's time to take the pilot and there we'd all go with him."

If that's funny to you it's because you know what I'm talking about. I was afraid. That's what it really boils down to. Fred-baby was afraid!

But I didn't know then what the Word said. And I wasn't doing what that Word said. So I had fear. But when I found out what that Word said, I found out I didn't have to be afraid.

FAITH IN ACTION...

at the Jordan River

II KINGS 5:1

1 Now Naaman, captain of the host of the king of Syria, was a great man with his master, and honourable, because by him the LORD had given deliverance unto Syria: he was a mighty man in valour, but he was a leper.

You can read the intervening verses to see how this Syrian captain happened to come to the prophet Elisha in Israel. We'll pick up with verse 8 here. Elisha the man of God is speaking:

II KINGS 5:8-12

8 . . . let him come now to me, and he shall know that there is a prophet in Israel.

9 So Naaman came with his horses and with his chariot, and stood at the door of the house of Elisha.

10 And Elisha sent a messenger unto him, saying, Go and wash in Jordan seven times, and thy flesh shall come again to thee, and thou shalt be clean.

11 But Naaman was wroth, and went away, and said, Behold, I thought, He will surely come out to me, and stand, and call on the name of the LORD his God, and strike his hand over the place, and recover the leper.

12 Are not Abana and Pharpar, rivers of Damascus, better than all the waters of Israel? may I not wash in them, and be clean? So he turned and went away in a rage.

We want to do it our way. He came. He wanted to be healed. He had an incurable disease. But he had his mind made up how it was going to work. That's how we do. We pray and we want God to answer it our way. But the mode of operation is irrelevant and immaterial. What counts is the end result. If I need $10,000 to take care of some business, I don't care if the man who brings that money to me is black or white. All I want is the money. If I'm hungry I don't care who's waiting the table. They can be big, fat, ugly, short, tall, bald-headed, or wearing a wig—it doesn't make me any difference. What I want is the food. But we want to limit God and put Him in our little cubicle, our little box, saying, "It has to be this way."

It's when you do what the Word says, and your faith is exercised, that God will vindicate that faith, and you'll get your answer.

Naaman went away in a rage. God had said by the prophet, "Go wash in the Jordan seven times." Dipping in the water seven times, that's about as stupid as going around the walls of Jericho. But remember what happened to those walls!

"We've toiled all night and taken nothing," Peter said. But a few minutes later the nets were breaking, as they tried to pull those fish in. All of a sudden things changed! Why?

Nevertheless, at thy Word. At thy Word. At thy Word. At thy Word.

Are you doing what the Word says?

II KINGS 5:13-14

13 And his servants came near, and spake unto him, and said, My father, if the prophet had bid thee do some great thing, wouldest thou not have done it? How much rather then, when he saith to thee, Wash, and be clean?
14 Then went he down, and dipped himself seven times in Jordan, according to the saying of the man of God: and his flesh came again like unto the flesh of a little child, and he was clean.

Notice he didn't get clean at the fifth dip. He didn't get clean at the sixth dip. He had to go in seven times.

You say, "Why seven times? Why not three?"

I don't know. But one thing I do know, when he came out that seventh time, brother, he wasn't a leper anymore!

He acted on the Word. *We've toiled all night and have taken nothing, NEVERTHELESS AT THY WORD* That's the secret.

Peter said, "Nevertheless at thy Word"—and the nets began to break. Israel was informed to walk around the wall seven times—which in the natural seemed foolish and a waste of time—but the walls fell down. Naaman, the leper—whom the prophet didn't even come out to see, but just sent a message out to him to dip seven times—came clean on the seventh dip. What did these do? They acted on the Word.

FAITH IN ACTION ...
at a marriage feast

JOHN 2:1-2
1 And the third day there was a marriage in Cana
of Galilee; and the mother of Jesus was there:
2 And both Jesus was called, and his disciples,
to the marriage.

You are familiar with the fact that they ran out of
wine for the feast. We'll read the account of what happened from there.

JOHN 2:6-10

6 And there were set six waterpots of stone, after
the manner of the purifying of the Jews, contain-
ing two or three firkins apiece.

7 Jesus saith unto them, Fill the waterpots with
water. And they filled them up to the brim.

8 And he saith unto them, Draw out now, and
bear unto the governor of the feast. And they
bare it.

9 When the ruler of the feast had tasted the water
that was made wine, and knew not whence it
was: (but the servants which drew the water
knew;) the governor of the feast called the bride-
groom.

10 And saith unto him, Every man at the beginning doth set forth good wine; and when men
have well drunk, then that which is worse; but
thou hast kept the good wine until now.

Jesus worked a miracle here. How did He work it?
By speaking a WORD. Yet there was required in the servants obedience to that Word. No miracle would have
transpired—no water would have turned into wine—if
they had not done what Jesus said. They acted on the
Word. That's what faith is—*ACTING ON THE WORD
OF GOD.*

When Jesus speaks, that's God speaking to you. And when He tells you to do something, if you'll do it, you'll reap the benefits. He said, "Fill them up with water."

I can imagine how the servants could have been like some of us, . . . "I ain't gonna waste my time filling these pots up with water. They're out of wine, not water. What's this joker talking about, fill them up with water? What's the matter with him?"

And then Jesus said—and this was the most audacious thing of all—"Draw some out now, and bear it to the governor of the feast."

The guy who's in charge of the feast! I can imagine the servants could have said, "Man, wait a minute! We just came off a strike last month. My kids need things. We were on that strike six weeks and I lost my wages all that time. Things are bad at home. The creditors are on my neck. If we fool around and take this water to the governor of the feast when they're out of wine, do you know what he's going to say to us, man? We'll be shopping for another job."

They could have said that in the natural, because it was ridiculous in the natural. *Take water and bear it to the governor of the feast?* But when they took out that water—while they were on their way—that water was changed into wine! How was it done? Through their acting on the Word.

Many times God's Word tells us to do something and in the natural it doesn't look like it's doing anything for us. But it is, if you'll stand in faith without wavering.

It amazes me how a farmer, with no more than nature as his guide line, can plant a seed, and though he can't even see the seed growing or germinating beneath the ground, he'll go ahead and hire the people he needs to harvest the crop. He'll figure out how many trucks he needs to take the crop from the field to the station, or wherever it's going. He'll make all those preparations without seeing a thing. He's not even going on the Word of God—just nature. Yet he'll act in faith.

But when it comes to us, who claim to be blood bought and blood washed, who say, "I believe it from Genesis to Revelation."

Are you afraid?

"Yes, pray for me."

Are you worried?

"Yes, I sure am. I don't know how I'm gonna pay these bills."

But you believe it from Genesis to Revelation. So DO IT! Don't tell me what you believe—DO IT.

Jesus said, *"Not every one that saith unto me, Lord, Lord, shall enter into the kingdom of heaven; but HE THAT DOETH THE WILL of my Father."* (Matthew 7:21). God's Word is His will. You can talk about it, sing about it, shout about it, dance about it, clap about it—and it will mean nothing, nothing, nothing—if you don't DO IT.

We've toiled all night and have taken nothing, nevertheless at thy Word.

FAITH IN ACTION ...

at the pool of Siloam

JOHN 9:1, 6-7a

1 And as Jesus passed by, he saw a man which was blind from his birth . . .

6 When he (Jesus) had thus spoken, he spat on the ground, and made clay of the spittle, and he anointed the eyes of the blind man with the clay,

7 And said unto him, Go, wash in the pool of Siloam . . .

That is the most ridiculous thing I ever heard of—spit on the ground—made some clay—put it on the man's eyes—then told him to go wash it off in the pool of Siloam.

He didn't say go down to the ocean. He didn't say go down to the sea. He said a specific place. He said, ". . . the pool of Siloam."

In the natural that is ridiculous. Why didn't He just pray over him? Why didn't He just lay hands on him and heal him? Why go through all this business about spitting on the ground—it's unsanitary, anyhow—and putting it on his eyes, and then making him go somewhere to wash it off? Why didn't He just speak the Word and heal him?

The man did what Jesus told him. I can imagine if he had run into some of us on the way to the pool.

"Hey man, where you going?"

Oh, I'm on my way cross town to the pool of Siloam."

"Say, what's that strange looking stuff on your eyes? What's that on your face there?"

"Well, I'll tell you. A man named Jesus spit on the ground, made some clay, put it on my eyes, and told me that if I'd go wash it off, I'd come seeing."

"Man, you ain't gonna fall for no mess like that are you? You mean you're gonna believe something like that? Are you that stupid? I wouldn't let Him make no fool out of me like that. 'Go wash it off in the pool of Siloam.' What kinda mess is that?"

We've toiled all night and taken nothing. . . .

But that man went to the pool of Siloam, and the Bible says that he came seeing!

Later on the Pharisees caught him and questioned him repeatedly. He replied to their interrogation, ". . . *one thing I know, that, whereas I was blind, now I see*" (John 9:25). Glory to God! Now I see!

How did he see? He acted on the Word of Jesus. Jesus said, "Go and wash it off."

"Yes, but that doesn't make sense."

It doesn't make any difference. He received his eyesight.

That's what holds many back. They don't want to be made a fool of.

"My friends will think I'm a nut. If I'm sitting up here and can't pay my rent and can't pay my taxes and they come to see me and ask how things are and I say, 'Praise the Lord all my needs are met,' they'll think I'm some kinda nut."

You'd rather have your needs unmet so all your friends will think you're just a regular fellow. You don't want to be called a nut. You don't want to be called a religious fanatic.

The man born blind was a religious fanatic, but he got his eyesight!

FAITH IN ACTION...

on a housetop

LUKE 5:17

17 And it came to pass on a certain day, as he was teaching, that there were Pharisees and doctors of the law sitting by, which were come out of every town of Galilee, and Judaea, and Jerusalem: and the power of the Lord was present to heal them.

That same power is present today. That same healing and miracle working power is present today.

LUKE 5:18-20, 24, 25

18 And, behold, men brought in a bed a man which was taken with a palsy: and they sought means to bring him in, and to lay him before him.

19 And when they could not find by what way they might bring him in because of the multitude, they went upon the housetop, and let him down through the tiling with his couch into the midst before Jesus.

20 And when he saw their faith, he said unto him, Man, thy sins are forgiven thee . . .

24 But that ye may know that the Son of man hath power upon earth to forgive sins, (he said unto the sick of the palsy,) I say unto thee, Arise, and take up thy couch, and go into thine house.

25 And immediately he rose up before them, and took up that whereon he lay, and departed to his own house, glorifying God.

Look at the 20th verse. *"And when he saw their faith. . . ."* Can you see faith? Show me faith. Put it in your hand and show it to me. What does faith look like? Can you see faith?

Not exactly. But you can see faith's actions.

THEY BROUGHT—four men brought on a couch— another man who was paralyzed and couldn't walk. They brought him there to be healed.

"And when he saw their faith. . . ." What did Jesus see? ACTIONS! Jesus saw their actions!

That's what faith is. *FAITH IS ACTING ON THE WORD OF GOD!*

Are you acting? Can the Lord see your faith?

FAITH IN ACTION ...

on a sabbath

LUKE 6:6-8a

6 And it came to pass also on another sabbath, that he entered into the synagogue and taught: and there was a man whose right hand was withered.

7 And the scribes and Pharisees watched him, whether he would heal on the sabbath day; that they might find an accusation against him.

8 But he knew their thoughts, and said to the man which had the withered hand, Rise up, and stand forth in the midst . . .

"Man, He ain't gonna make no fool out of me. Stand up in the midst?"

LUKE 6:8b-10a

8 . . . and he arose and stood forth.

9 Then said Jesus unto them, I will ask you one thing; Is it lawful on the sabbath days to do good, or to do evil? to save life, or to destroy it?

10 And looking round about upon them all, he said unto the man, Stretch forth thy hand . . .

"Yes, but I can't stretch forth my hand. Don't you know my hand is withered? I can't stretch my hand forth! Are you trying to make a fool out of me before all these people? Why would you tell me to do something like that? I've been crippled like this all my life—and you're telling me to stretch my hand forth?"

We have toiled all night and have taken nothing. . . .

LUKE 6:10

10 And looking round about upon them all, he said unto the man, Stretch forth thy hand. And

he did so: and his hand was restored whole as the other.

NEVERTHELESS AT THY WORD! This man stretched out his hand. He acted on the Word of Jesus. He did the impossible. He did that which defied logic and reasoning. He acted on that Word. And it wasn't until he acted that the power of God was activated in his life.

Many of us are waiting for God to work a miracle or give us a healing, and then we'll believe it. But, you see, you have to believe you have it NOW, ACT like it's true, and then the power of God comes.

LUKE 6:46

46 And why call ye me, Lord, Lord, and do not the things which I say?

Here we see DOING again. ACTING on the Word.

In Luke 7:1-10 we have the account of the centurion's faith. His servant was sick. Jesus said, "I'll come and heal him."

The centurion said, *"Lord, trouble not thyself: for I am not worthy that thou shouldest enter under my roof: ... BUT SAY IN A WORD, and my servant shall be healed"* (Luke 7:6-7).

Jesus turned to the crowd and said, "I have not found so great faith, no, not in Israel." (Verse 9)

What did Jesus mean?

The man had said in effect, "Your Word is enough. Just your Word. All you have to do is say the Word and it will be done."

The centurion was a man in authority. He knew that when he gave a soldier a command, that was it. He did it. His word had authority. And he knew Jesus was a Man of authority, and that when Jesus spoke the Word, that was all that was necessary. That all Jesus had to say was, "Be healed."

He believed that, and he acted on it. He said, "Just speak the word only. All I need is your word."

Jesus gave him the Word. The healing took place. And Jesus remarked, "I have not found so great faith."

What was the faith? The man acknowledged the power and authority of the Word of God. Then he acted on it by going on home.

LUKE 8:19-21

19 Then came to him his mother and his brethren, and could not come at him for the press.

20 And it was told by certain which said, Thy mother and thy brethren stand without, desiring to see thee.

21 And he answered and said unto them, My mother and my brethren are these which hear the word of God, and do it.

Not, hear the word and talk about it. Not, hear it and sing about it. But, hear it and DO IT. *FAITH IS ACTING ON THE WORD OF GOD.*

Part IV

10

THE GOD KIND OF FAITH...What is it?

MARK 11:12-14

12 And on the morrow, when they were come from Bethany, he was hungry:

13 And seeing a fig tree afar off having leaves, he came, if haply he might find any thing thereon: and when he came to it, he found nothing but leaves; for the time of figs was not yet.

14 And Jesus answered and said unto it, No man eat fruit of thee hereafter for ever. And his disciples heard it.

Pay special attention to that last sentence. Underline it. Put parentheses around it. It's a very important statement. *"And his disciples HEARD it."*

They heard Jesus speak to this inanimate fig tree. Jesus spoke to a tree.

Now we must qualify something else here, because it seems as though Jesus did something uncouth, unorthodox, and unkind, to say the least. And that is, to come to a fig tree and expect to find fruit on it when there wasn't supposed to be any fruit. And then to curse the poor thing because it didn't have any fruit.

Jesus was not ignorant. He was born and raised in that part of the world. He'd lived there all His life, over 30 years. I would think He would know which trees should have fruit and which ones shouldn't have fruit. And that He would not have wasted His time going to a tree which He knew — by virtue of the fact He was born and raised in that part of the country –– wouldn't have any fruit on it.

There was more than one kind of fig tree. Some trees bore fruit all year long. Some trees bore fruit periodically. Those which had leaves on them were supposed to have fruit.

For some reason, this tree didn't have any fruit. And Jesus used it as an object lesson to teach what I believe is the most important lesson in the Bible concerning faith. And it's tied up with that statement — *and his disciples heard it.*

That means Jesus spoke out loud. Audibly. He committed Himself, in other words. He actually set Himself up for ridicule.

It would have been very easy for someone in the crowd to say, "This guy must be going off the deep end. Talking to a tree!" They call us fanatics for going to church more than once a week. What must they have thought of Jesus talking to a tree!

We're not going to read verses 15 through 19. They have no bearing upon what we're talking about in verses 12-14 and then in verse 20. What happens in between is somewhat parenthetical.

One morning Jesus was on His way into the city of Jerusalem to teach in the temple. On His way there He was hungry. He saw a fig tree. He came to it. There was no fruit. He cursed the tree. He went on into the city of Jerusalem.

That afternoon He walked back out to Bethany — passed by the tree –– and went on to Bethany.

The next morning He came back again on the same journey into Jerusalem. These intervening verses (15-19) tell what happened at the temple, which is not relevant to our story.

MARK 11:20-24

20 And in the morning, as they passed by, they

saw the fig tree dried up from the roots.

21 And Peter calling to remembrance saith unto him, Master, behold, the fig tree which thou cursedst is withered away.

22 And Jesus answering saith unto them, Have faith in God.

23 For verily I say unto you, That whosoever shall say unto this mountain, Be thou removed, and be thou cast into the sea; and shall not doubt in his heart, but shall believe that those things which he saith shall come to pass; he shall have whatsoever he saith.

24 Therefore I say unto you, What things soever ye desire, when ye pray, believe that ye receive them, and ye shall have them.

Peter said, "Lord, the fig tree is dried up."

Jesus took the opportunity to teach one of the most provocative and most profound lessons about faith. If you can ever learn this lesson . . . if you can ever really grasp it . . . I mean, get it past the block of ice sitting between your shoulder blades, and get it down into your spirit, into your heart . . . your troubles in life are over.

I'm not saying the enemy won't attack you. What I'm saying is, you can say, "Stop in the name of Jesus." And you can become ruler of your circumstances rather than the victim.

Jesus said, in the 22nd verse, *"Have faith in God."* In the literal Greek that statement should be rendered, *"Have the faith of God."* Or, in the vernacular of today, *"Have the God kind of faith."*

Why distinguish the God kind of faith? Because there are two kinds of faith in existence in the world.

    1. Natural human faith.

    2. Spiritual faith. Or, the God kind of faith.

Many born again Christians, even many who have been filled with the Spirit and speak with other tongues, have not learned how to exercise the God kind of faith. They are still living their lives, still praying to God, and still expecting to get answers, based upon the mankind of faith.

The man kind of faith says, "I will believe it when I see it. I will believe it when I feel it. I will believe it when I hear something. When I see something. When God gives me a sign. Then I will believe it."

That's the human kind of faith — the man kind — and you'll never get one prayer answered using that kind of faith. You'll never get healed from any sickness or disease using the man kind of faith which says, "I'll believe it WHEN I see it."

The God kind of faith says, "I believe it, therefore I WILL see it." The God kind of faith believes first of all, and then confesses with the mouth what it believes.

Jesus was a Man who used the God kind of faith. A Man who did things which in the natural were very ridiculous, even things that would bring Him up for ridicule. On one occasion He had the audacity to talk to the wind. How ridiculous can you get? But the peculiar thing about it is, either the wind, or whatever was behind the wind, heard what He said. Because the wind obeyed! On another occasion He talked to the water. He told it to lie down and be quiet. The peculiar thing is, it obeyed Him! In our passage He talked to an inanimate tree. Twenty-four hours later they saw the tree dried up from the roots! On several occasions Jesus stretched the imagination to its limit and even dared to talk to dead bodies — and they heard Him and obeyed!

But notice that He SAID something.

Concerning the fig tree Mark 11:14 says, *"And his disciples heard it."* He spoke out loud. He committed Himself. He confessed with His mouth what He believed in His heart. He believed that when He spoke to that tree, the tree would obey Him. It would dry up. And he dared to speak to it.

Do you have that kind of faith in the Word of God? Do you believe when you tell a fever to leave that it's going to go? Do you believe when you say my needs are met in Jesus Christ, that they are met?

The God kind of faith does. The God kind of faith says, "I believe it. Therefore I confess it with my mouth. I say it. I commit myself. I put myself out on a limb. Because I believe it."

What is the God kind of faith?

The God kind of faith (1) *believes* in the heart, and (2) *confesses* with the mouth. Those two things have to go together. Many believe, but they won't confess anything.

And when I say "confess" I mean "say." I'm not talking about confessing sin, or wrong, or failure, or the fact you've missed the mark. I'm talking about a *positive* confession.

Many believe and say, "Oh yes, I believe God. I know God can heal. I know the Lord can do anything. Yes sir, I believe the Bible."

Do you believe the Word?

"Oh yes, I believe the Bible. I've believed the Bible ever since I was a little boy when I sat at Grandmother's knee and she used to read Bible stories to me about Daniel in the lion's den, and Jonah and the whale. Oh yes, I believe the Bible from Genesis to Revelation."

Do you believe you are healed?

"No!"

Did you know the Bible which you believe from Genesis to Revelation says that with His stripes ye were healed?

"Yes. But I don't feel like I'm healed."

See the difference? Feel. Feel. Feel! "I don't *feel* like it. I don't *see* it."

The God kind of faith believes it, and says it, *without seeing anything*. That tree didn't dry up right away. It wasn't until 24 hours later that they saw the tree was dried up from the roots. They had to pass by that same tree on their way back to Bethany after Jesus had cursed the tree that morning. Apparently there was no visible change in the tree. It wasn't until 24 hours later that Peter noticed the tree was dried up. Jesus spoke that Word. It was the Word of faith. It was the God kind of faith in manifestation.

11

THE GOD KIND OF FAITH... *at creation*

HEBREWS 11:3

3 Through faith we understand that the worlds
were framed by the word of God, so that things
which are seen were not made of things which
do appear.

*"Through faith we understand that the worlds were
framed by the word of God. . . ."* This is not just saying
that by an exercise of our faith we believe that God spoke
the worlds into existence. It is saying that, but it's also
saying much more. It's telling us how God did it! By using
His faith! Not with bricks, wood, mortar, or any such
thing. He did it with His faith.

Yes, God has faith. And He uses it. If he didn't, how
could we have His kind?

God operates on the God kind of faith. What other
kind of faith could God use but the God kind?

God believed in His heart that what He said with
His mouth would come to pass, and He dared to say it.
In the presence of the angels, of Satan, of everything then
in existence, God stepped out on space and said, "Let
there be."

When we read the first chapter of Genesis—which is
not really a story of creation but of restoration, restoring
the earth to its original condition, but that's another subject—I want you to notice a few words in particular.

I used to read that first chapter of Genesis and think,
"This almost sounds like a fairy tale, the way the words
are put together."

I don't mean a fairy tale in the sense it is untrue or
make-believe, but in the almost childlike way it's worded.
For instance, Genesis 1:3, *"And God said. . . ."* Verse 6,

"And God said. . . ." Verse 9, *"And God said. . . ."* Verse 11, *"And God said. . . ."* Verse 14, *"And God said. . . ."* Verse 20, *"And God said. . . ."* Verse 24, verse 26, and verse 29, *"And God said . . . And God said . . . And God said. . . ."*

"How childish," I thought. It didn't appear to me that an intelligent being had done this. Had I had been writing it, as any intelligent being would have, I would have written it like this: In the beginning God created the heaven and the earth! (1) The sun. (2) The moon. (3) The stars. (4) The dry land. Etc., etc. That would have told us exactly what had been created and we could have dispensed with all that repetition . . . And God said . . . And God said . . . And God said. . . .

One day the Spirit of God revealed to me the "why" of this. He showed me why God put these things in the Word. He said them for our benefit. He said them to show us how the God kind of faith works.

GENESIS 1:3

3 And God said, Let there be light: . . .

God could have just made the light without saying anything. Why didn't He just make light? Why didn't the writer just say, "And God made the light." Wouldn't that have told us what happened? It would have told us about the light. And it would have told us God made it.

But it doesn't say that. It says, *"And God said. . . ."*

Why?

Because that's the way the God kind of faith works. You have to say it first. You have to believe in your heart that what you say with your mouth will come to pass, and then dare to say it. That's how the God kind of faith works.

"That doesn't make sense," you say.

You're right. It doesn't. It's not sense—it's faith. "Sense" is not in any of the verses we've read thus far.

Jesus didn't say, Have the God kind of sense. He said, "Have the God kind of faith."

"And God said, Let there be light. . . ."

Then what happened?

". . . and there was light."

But notice when the light came. The light did not come until after God spoke. God must have first of all believed in His heart that what He said with His mouth would come to pass; otherwise, there would have been no reason for Him to say it. But that's how the God kind of faith works, and it has to work that same way for you.

"Yes, but I'm not God."

The Bible says that if you have been born again and have received Jesus Christ as Saviour you're a son of God.

If you have children, you might try to say one is not your child, but if you disect that child, there's some of you in him. There's some of your husband or wife in him. Whatever you are, that's what the child is.

If our Father is a faith God, then we must be faith children of a faith God. If we're children of God, we ought to act like our Father. We ought to exercise the same kind of faith our Father exercises.

GENESIS 1:6
6 And God said, Let there be a firmament in the midst of the waters. . . .

"And God said"—there it is again. And again. And again. In verses 9, and 11, and 14, and 20, and 24, and 26, and 29. But notice that nothing came into manifestation, nothing came into being, until AFTER GOD SAID IT.

That's a revelation. If you can just grasp it, your problems would be over. Just grasp the truth that it won't come—until after you say it. And you can't say it until you first of all believe it. That's just how it works. It's just that simple. The God kind of faith works by believing with the heart and confessing with the mouth.

Do you believe all your needs are met? Do you believe you're healed in your body? Do you believe you have divine health? Do you believe it? Can you say it? Can you confess it?

"I sure would like to!"

He never said anything about "like to." He said "do it." Then it becomes yours!

12

THE GOD KIND OF FAITH...is yours

Would you like to have the God kind of faith? Would you like to have the kind of faith Jesus had?

Somebody says, "Oh, I hope I can have that kind of faith. I'm just a-hopin' and a-prayin' God will give me that kind of faith."

That won't work. You'll never get any faith praying for it, or fasting for it, or hoping for it. It doesn't come that way.

If you're a believer, if you've been born again, YOU ALREADY HAVE THE GOD KIND OF FAITH. You already have it.

You may not be using it. You may be leaving it in the dresser drawer or locked up in a closet somewhere. And of course, that's why it's not working on your behalf. But if you're a Christian you have the God kind of faith.

Some people don't believe that. They'll say, "I don't have that kind of faith. I wish I did. But I don't."

If you've been born again, you have it. If you don't have it, you haven't been born again. You'd better get born again so you can get it.

"Yes, but I don't feel like I have it."

It has nothing to do with your feeling like it. It's so because God said it's so, not because you feel like it.

ROMANS 12:3
3 For I say, through the grace given unto me, to every man that is among you, not to think of himself more highly than he ought to think; but to think soberly, according as God hath dealt to every man the measure of faith.

We have to qualify that "every man" here is not every man in the world. It's every man in the church of Jesus

Christ, every man in the body of Christ at Rome. That's who Paul was writing to. This is what you call rightly dividing the Word, not wrongly dividing.

Many people read the Bible and when they see a word such as *everybody* or *every man,* they think it means every man in the world. But it must be qualified by the context in which the statement is found. Romans 12:3 is not saying every man in the world has faith.

Paul makes it plain in the first chapter of Romans that he's writing, *"To all that be in Rome, beloved of God, called to be saints...."* (Verse 7).

It is by faith that we are saved. So if we're in the body of Christ, whether we're in Rome, or Corinth, or Thessalonica, or Los Angeles, or New York City, we're in the same church, the same body, and we have the same Head over us, Jesus Christ. And we have the same Heavenly Father. That means He must deal to me the same measure of faith He dealt those people in Rome, otherwise He becomes a respecter of persons. But His Word says He has dealt to every man among us the measure of faith.

Let's look at another scripture that shows Paul is talking in Romans about every man in the body of Christ. Everybody in the world doesn't have faith—that is, the God kind.

II THESSALONIANS 3:2
2 And that we may be delivered from unreasonable and wicked men: for all men have not faith.

We need to understand how to qualify these things because that's how some smart alecs come up and say, "The Bible contradicts itself." They read in Romans, "God has dealt to every man the measure of faith," and then they come over and read where everybody doesn't have faith. That would be a contradiction if it were talking about the same thing, but it's not. You have to measure it by the context.

He's talking in one place about one kind of individual and in another place about another kind of individual. It is not a contradiction. In II Thessalonians He is not talking about men in Christ, but about those in the world. And they do not have the God kind of faith. They are not children of God—therefore they don't have His nature—therefore they couldn't have His kind of faith.

How Do We Get It?

ROMANS 12:3
3 . . . according as God hath dealt to every man the measure of faith.

How do we get the God kind of faith?

GOD HAS DEALT IT TO US.

EPHESIANS 2:8-9
8 For by grace are ye saved through faith; and that not of yourselves: it is the gift of God:
9 Not of works, lest any man should boast.

The gift here is twofold. Salvation itself is a gift. But also the faith by which you become saved is a gift God has to give you.

"Not of works. . . ." You can't work up this kind of faith. Some try to. They dance a little, run up and down the aisles of the church, and when they get that certain feeling, they feel like they have faith. That's not the way it comes.

"For by grace—grace is unmerited divine favor—*are ye saved through faith; and that*—that faith—*not of yourselves: IT IS THE GIFT OF GOD."*

We just read where Romans 12:3 says, *"God has dealt to every man the measure of faith."* It didn't say He sold it to us. It said He *dealt* it to us. He *gave* it to us.

What is the channel by which it comes? How did the grace of God come to us. How do we discover we are lost? How do we discover Jesus died for us? How do we discover Jesus rose from the dead?

The Bible tells us how faith comes, and this is the only way you can get it, friend. You can't get it by tarrying. You can't get it at the mourners bench. You can't get it by fasting or by tithing. You can only get it by receiving it as a free handout from God. Now how does God hand it out to you?

ROMANS 10:17

17 So then faith cometh by hearing, and hearing by the word of God.

That's how it comes. And the only way you'll get it. *Faith comes by hearing—and hearing by the Word of God.*

The reason most congregations don't have any more faith than they do in manifestation is they never hear the Word of God. They hear junk. Emotionalism. Sensationalism. Politics. Prose. Theology. You have to preach the Word of God to get faith into people. The preaching of the Word of God is how faith comes.

Now you can understand and appreciate Jesus' command to, *"Go ye into all the world, and preach the gospel to every creature."*

"Why, Jesus?"

"Because faith comes by hearing and hearing by the Word of God. If you don't go and preach the Word, faith can't come. If faith doesn't come, they can't believe. If they can't believe, they can't get saved. If they don't get saved, they will die and go to hell. So you go preach the Gospel to them, and faith will come, and they can believe in Me as Saviour, and pass from spiritual death into spiritual life."

Faith comes by hearing, and hearing by the Word of God.

Not only is this true relative to salvation, but in every other area of our spiritual life. I know this to be true, not only scripturally, but also experientially.

Before we started Crenshaw Christian Center, I pastored a church for eight and one-half years. For the first five years, we never had one manifestation of any gift of the Holy Spirit. No one was ever divinely healed. No miracles ever took place. Not one person was ever filled with the Holy Spirit, speaking with other tongues. However, many people were saved on a regular basis.

Do you know why?

Because this preacher preached salvation messages. Therefore there was faith in the congregation for salvation. But we never had any of the other things for the simple reason this preacher never preached or taught on them. There was no faith in the congregation for those things.

Do you know why many people in many denominations do not believe in divine healing, miracles, the baptism with the Holy Spirit, speaking with other tongues?

It's not really that they *don't* believe, it's that they *can't* believe, because there is no faith for these things in most of their congregations. Their pastors are not preaching and teaching on these aspects of the Gospel. Consequently, there is no faith for them.

"So then faith cometh by hearing, and hearing by the word of God" (Romans 10:17).

I know this to be a fact, because when I was filled with the Holy Spirit in 1970, speaking with other tongues, and the Spirit began to teach me the Word along the lines

of faith and the *full gospel*, I immediately began to preach
and teach on the baptism with the Holy Spirit, speaking
with other tongues, gifts of the Spirit, divine healing,
miracles. And from that day up to this writing we never
have a week go by in our church where these things are
not manifested. Why? Because I'm preaching and teaching
the Word on these issues, and faith comes by hearing and
hearing by the Word of God.

13

THE GOD KIND OF FAITH ... in your heart and in your mouth

ROMANS 10:8
8 But what saith it? The word is nigh thee, even in thy mouth, and in thy heart: that is, the word of faith, which we preach:

What a strange place for the Word to be. The Word is near you, it says, even in your mouth. What's it in your mouth for? To confess it! To say it!

Jesus spoke to the tree *and His disciples heard it.* In Genesis it's recorded, *"And God said. . . ."* The Word was in His mouth. He said it. He confessed it.

And that's what you have to do. You have to get His Word into your heart, then put it in your mouth and start saying it. When you start saying it, then it will start working on your behalf.

". . . The word is nigh thee, even in thy mouth, and in thy heart: . . ." What word? *"THE WORD OF FAITH, which we preach:"*

The Word causes faith to come, that's why it's called *the word of faith.* You have to believe it, then put it in your mouth and say it.

Romans 10:8 says the very same thing Jesus said in Mark 11:23. Jesus said, *". . . whosoever shall SAY unto this mountain, Be thou removed, and be thou cast into the sea; and shall not doubt in his heart, but shall believe that those things which he SAITH shall come to pass; he shall have whatsoever he SAITH"* (Mark 11:23). And Romans 10:8 says the same thing. It's saying to us that the Word is in our mouth.

"Well what am I supposed to do with it? Gargle with it?"

No! SAY IT! Speak it out. When you speak it out, things will begin to happen on your behalf.

ROMANS 10:9-10
9 That if thou shalt confess with thy mouth the Lord Jesus, and shalt believe in thine heart that God hath raised him from the dead, thou shalt be saved.
10 For with the heart man believeth unto righteousness; and with the mouth confession is made unto salvation.

That's how the sinner takes the Word of God and creates the reality of salvation in his life, by believing in his heart that God raised Him from the dead, and then by confessing Jesus as Lord.

Jesus said, *"Whosoever therefore shall confess me before men, him will I confess also before my Father which is in heaven"* (Matthew 10:32).

You have to SAY it. Some want to be secret disciples. They'll never make it in. You have to SAY it. You have to put yourself on the spot. You have to put yourself up for ridicule. They may say you're nuts. They may call you a fanatic. But that's what it takes. You have to confess it.

Look at verse 10 with me.

"For with the heart man believeth . . ." (That's with the spirit. The heart is the spirit.)

"For with the heart man believeth unto righteousness; and with the mouth (there's that mouth again) *confession is made unto salvation."*

This 10th verse is in reality a formula which will work for you in every area of your life. It is the key to receiving the blessings of God. This formula is: (1) BELIEVING IT IN THE HEART AND (2) CONFESSING IT WITH THE MOUTH. That's the combination which opens the lock!

"For with the heart man believeth." Not with the mind, not with your brain. Sometimes our brains get in

the way. We're not putting a premium on ignorance, but sometimes our minds do get in the way. For it is with the heart man believes, relative to the things of God.

You don't believe God with your human intellect, your human mind. You believe God with your heart, your spirit, the man on the inside, the man who's been born again. And until you learn how to understand and respond to God from your spirit, you'll be second-rate as a Christian. Spiritually you'll be second-rate.

Notice the wording, *"For with the heart man believeth UNTO. . . ."* You can drop the word *righteousness* and put in anything else you want to. You can put a mountain in there if you want to, because Jesus said, *"Whosoever shall say unto this mountain . . . and shall not doubt in his heart, but shall believe. . . ."*

You can drop *righteousness* because this is a formula. Paul just happens to be talking about salvation in this scripture, so he uses righteousness. But you could put anything in there you want—healing, your needs met, new job, car, home, whatever you need.

"For with the heart man believeth . . . (you have to believe it with your heart) *and with the mouth confession is made unto. . . ."* You have to (1) BELIEVE it and (2) SAY it.

That's what God did. He believed in His heart that what He said with His mouth would come to pass, and He said it. He said, "Let there be light." And there it was!

Jesus believed in His heart that when He spoke to the tree it would obey Him. He spoke to it out loud. His disciples heard Him. And the tree dried up. He spoke to fevers and they left. He spoke to pain and it obeyed. He spoke to demons and they left. He believed in His heart and He said it with His mouth. That's the key!

If Christians can get to that point where they believe and confess, you talk about power being manifested, we haven't seen anything yet!

How We Hear

Faith comes by hearing and hearing by the Word of God. And Jesus warned, *"Take heed therefore how ye hear. . . .* (Luke 8:18)." Be careful about how you hear. It's important.

Why?

If you don't hear right, you'll miss faith. And if you miss faith, you'll miss God. And if you miss God, you'll get nothing.

Somebody says, "I don't understand why God won't save So-and-so. I don't understand why God won't heal So-and-so. I don't understand why God won't deliver So-and-so."

For your information, He already has! He's already saved everybody He's going to save. He's already healed everybody He's going to heal.

Somebody says, "When were you saved?"

"Oh, I was saved January the 14th, 19-so-and-so."

No you weren't. You were saved 1900 years ago at Calvary. Right then God saw everybody saved who's ever going to be saved. What happened on January 14th, 19-so-and-so is the reality of salvation became yours personally when you by faith received it. But God didn't just save you then. You were already saved. You just didn't know it. God doesn't save anybody the minute somebody walks down the aisle. They were already saved. What they're doing now is entering into the reality of it in a personal way.

Salvation belongs to everybody. (II Corinthians 5:19) Every man in the world has a right to be saved. It's God's will that everybody be saved. God is not interested in anybody going to hell. Hell wasn't even prepared for man in the first place. The Bible says it was prepared for the devil and his angels. God doesn't want you going there.

(Did you know it's harder to get into hell than into heaven? You have to do something to go to hell. You have to spit in God's eye, trample the blood of Christ under your feet, and reject Him as your personal Saviour. You have to do away with all the songs ever sung about Jesus and the fact that He saves. You'd have to in effect burn down every church. Kill every minister. Get rid of every missionary and all the material ever written about Christ and the things of God. That's what you're actually doing when you go to hell. You're rejecting all that. Getting rid of all that. And all you have to do is say, "Yes, Jesus," and you can go to heaven. Praise God!)

"Why won't God save? Why won't God heal?"

He already has. The Bible says that with His stripes YOU WERE HEALED. (I Peter 2:24) That means you are healed. Now!

The Bible says that He *HAS* delivered us from the kingdom of darkness. Darkness is Satan's kingdom. We've been delivered from Satan's kingdom and dominion. He has no *legal* right to hold us in bondage. I am already delivered. (Colossians 1:13)

All I have to do is stand up on my rights and say, "Satan, take your hands off my life, off my family, off my finances, off everything that belongs to me, because I have been set free by Jesus. I'm free NOW—not next year! *NOW* I'm free, because Jesus has set me free.

But I have to *believe* that and *confess* that, or it won't work for me.

That's how I stay well. I'll never be sick. It's the most thrilling exciting thing to know that I'm going to live way past 70 years old and never be sick. That blows my mind. I'll never spend a dime for medicine. Never give a doctor a dollar. Never have to go to a pharmacist. Glory to God— I'll NEVER be sick!

I believe that in my heart and I'm saying it with my mouth. Jesus said if I'd believe it in my heart and say it with my mouth, I could have it.

And the reason I can have it is, when He died on Calvary, He healed me then. ". . . *Himself took our infirmities, and bare our sicknesses*" (Matthew 8:17). "*. . . by whose stripes ye WERE healed*" (I Peter 2:24). The Bible says that. It also says the Word is nigh me, even in my mouth. So I just start saying, "Praise God, I'm healed."

When the devil comes and trys to put a symptom on me, I say, "You can't put that on me. I'm healed. Didn't you know that? Read the Bible, devil. I'm healed."

I'll never be sick—praise God forever more! That's glorious news to never be sick. I'll live to a ripe old age, if Jesus tarries. And I won't be weak and senile, but strong and virile. It's exciting news for me never to have to worry about being sick. When they tell me another flu epidemic has come in, I just laugh at it. It's not for me. It doesn't have my name on the package. I refuse to receive it.

Now, when I say I'll never be sick, that doesn't mean Satan won't try to put something on me. But when he comes to deliver his package of symptoms, I just don't sign for the package. I don't accept the subpoena.

"How do you sign for the package, Brother Price?"

By believing in your heart and saying with your mouth, "I think I'm gonna be sick." Remember Jesus said in Mark 11:23 that if you believe it in your heart and say it with your mouth, you'll have what you say.

The reason many haven't received anything from God is, they won't believe it and won't confess it. They'll whine and cry, beg and plead. They'll do everything else except believe God and confess it with their mouth. They're waiting to feel some dumb feeling.

"Well, I know the Lord was here, I felt Him."

You didn't feel the Lord. That was some emotion you felt. You can't feel God. You feel things in the sense world. But you don't feel God. God is a Spirit. Jesus said you worship God in spirit and in truth. You sense His presence with your spirit.

"Oh, if I only had enough faith."

You have it. You already have it. If you don't, you're not saved. God has dealt to every one of us the measure of faith. It's a gift.

How did it come? By hearing.

Where is it? In your heart and in your mouth.

All you have to do is start opening your mouth and start saying—confessing—with your mouth what you really believe.

Some don't say it because they don't really believe it. If they did, they'd stop belly-aching and crying, and would start saying what God says. They'd start saying:

"I am a conqueror!" (Romans 8:37) "I can do all things through Christ who strengthens me! (Philippians 4:13)

"I don't have to bow down to the devil or anything he has to dish out. I'm a child of the King. I'll live like a king. I'll look like a king. And I'll act like a king."

The Measure

Somebody says, "Oh, if I only had enough faith."

If you know Jesus Christ as your personal Saviour, then you are right now a believer. And you have all the faith you're ever going to need.

"Yes, but that measure sure sounds like it's just a little bit. I must not have too much."

The things God gives are so potent He only has to give you a little bit. You don't need much. The measure God gives you goes a long way.

MATTHEW 17:20

20 And Jesus said unto them, Because of your unbelief: for verily I say unto you, If ye have faith as a grain of mustard seed, ye shall say unto this mountain, Remove hence to yonder place; and it shall remove; and nothing shall be impossible unto you.

That's how big the measure is—mustard seed size. You know how big a mustard seed is. Some people wear them around their necks in small magnified glass balls.

And Jesus said a mustard seed size would move 29,000 foot Mount Everest.

"Yes, but He didn't mean a literal mountain."

That's just why the mountain has never moved for you—you don't believe it.

"Do you mean to tell me you believe that?"

I certainly do. I believe that if I get into a situation where I have to have a mountain moved, that mountain will move. If it doesn't move, then the Bible is untrue. Now, you can't just run out and grab a mountain and say, "All right, mountain, move," not really believing it, and testing God to see if it will work. That's not faith. But, I believe if I get into a situation where I have to have a mountain move, that mountain will go.

Words

Words dominate us. We've been talking about what we confess, what we say with our mouth. Words dominate us. Whether they're positive or negative, words will control your life.

"Thou art snared with the words of thy mouth, thou art taken with the words of thy mouth" (Proverbs 6:2). Snared. A snare is a trap. A trap to catch animals. Your words will ensnare you. Whether you say positive words, or negative words, those words will rule your life.

Who dominates your mind?

Does doubt and fear? defeat? unbelief? failure? "I can't make it"? "I'm not good enough"?

If that dominates your daily thoughts, you have a mind dominated by the devil. Anything that's of doubt is of Satan. Everything of God is positive. Everything in Christ is *yea and amen*. Everything in the devil is, well, maybe, if, it might be, perhaps, it could be, there's a chance. All that kind of talk is of the devil. He'll feed that garbage into your mind and you'll pick it up and start saying, "Well, you never know what God is going to do. Maybe it'll work and maybe it won't."

That's just why it won't work. That's not faith. It's doubt. And doubt is the thief of God's greater blessings.

No! Praise God! You can have what you say, if you dare to believe it. Start confessing these positive things. And I'm not talking about the power of positive thinking. I'm talking about the power of positive confession in line with the written, revealed Word of the Living God. Start saying, "I am a victor. I am a conqueror. I am healed. I am a believer. I am not a doubter. I have a measure of the God kind of faith."

"Well," somebody says, "Mark 11:23 is not for us today."

Yes it is. Jesus said "whosoever" shall say unto this mountain. That "whosoever" is the same Greek word as the "whosoever" in John 3:16. If John 3:16 is for us today, then Mark 11:23 is for us today.

And somebody says, "I'm just not good enough. I'm just not worthy enough. I don't believe God's going to heal me."

You're just believing the devil's lie. The devil has you right where he wants you, in his hip pocket.

II CORINTHIANS 5:17
17 Therefore if any man be in Christ he is a new creature: old things are passed away; behold, all things are become new.

If you say you're unworthy, not good enough, a failure, and all of that, you're talking about God's fair creation. Do you mean to tell me that God is in the business of making *failure* new creatures?

You were unworthy, that's why you needed to get saved. But do you mean to tell me that after you're saved you're still unworthy? God didn't do too much for you then, did He?

You hadn't thought of that, had you? And when you're belly-aching and crying, you think you're being humble and don't know you're being ignorant. Crying, coming down to every altar call, whining and confessing how poor you are, how weak you are, how unworthy you are, and while you're down there kneeling, the devil's standing over you with his foot on your neck crying, "Fool!"

(You don't hear him, but that's what he's saying.)

"Fool, dummy, you don't know you're a conqueror. And look at me, I've got my foot on your neck."

The Bible says I am a new creature. I am a brand new man. I'm not what I used to be. Glory to God. I'm a new creature in Christ Jesus. I have the power of God in my life. I have the blood of Christ that's my undergirding. I don't have to be afraid of the circumstances of life. I don't take any fear tactics from the devil. When he tries to bring fear tactics on me, I say, "I don't receive that. It's not mine. It doesn't belong to me and I don't have to receive it."

*   *   *

Remember this, your faith will never register above the words of your lips. Whatever you confess with your mouth, is exactly where your faith is going to register and operate. If you confess negativism and doubt and unbelief, that's what you're going to have. Your faith won't rise any higher than the words of your mouth.

If you confess failure, doubt, weakness, inability, then that's what you'll have. But when you start confessing, "Praise God, I am a conqueror. Praise God, my needs are met. Praise God, I am healed. Praise God, I have divine health. Praise God I will rule as a king in life," then that's what you'll start having.

The God kind of faith believes in the heart that what it says with the mouth will come to pass, and then dares to say it!

Part V

14

How To Receive The Promises Of God By Faith

Keep in mind that things in the natural operate by principles. For instance, 2 + 2 = 4, 12 inches = 1 foot, etc., etc.

So it is in the realm of the spirit, in the realm of God. There are principles which operate in the realm of faith. To be consistently successful, relative to the things of God, one must know and understand how the principles of faith operate.

In our previous chapters, we have dealt with these principles of faith. What it is. What it isn't. Who has it. How it works. If a person will give diligent attention to what has been taught, he can be a winner in the game of life.

The purpose of this final chapter is to put the principles we've studied into a working formula which can be grasped and utilized by the average Christian. It will show you *how* to make a claim on the promises of God and *how* to make and maintain a proper confession until the claim is manifested in the physical realm.

It must be understood from the beginning that these principles and formulas will not work for a person deliberately living in open sin and rebellion against the revealed will of God as presented in His Word. If you know to do a certain thing the Word tells you, and you deliberately and willfully disobey the injunction of the Word, your faith will not and cannot work in that environment. Living in disobedience to the Word will nullify your faith.

So it is assumed you are living in line with the Word of God to the best of your knowledge and ability. If this assumption is correct, there is no reason in the world for your faith to fail to work for you in every area and aspect of life.

How To Receive Material Things
...finances, for instance

Let's take the problem of finances as a starter. Let's say you need $500 to pay your property taxes, and you don't have enough money left out of your weekly pay check after all your regular bills are paid.

A. FIND THE SCRIPTURES WHICH PROMISE YOU THE THING YOU NEED OR DESIRE.

Faith must always be based on God's Word. Relative to finances we could use such scriptures as: Philippians 4:19; II Corinthians 8:9; III John 2; Mark 11:24.

B. THE PRAYER: (THE CLAIMING OF THE PROMISE OF GOD RELATIVE TO YOUR PARTICULAR NEED.)

Heavenly Father,
I thank you for your Word.
And your Word declares in Philippians 4:19, "*But my God shall supply all your need according to his riches in glory by Christ Jesus.*"
This is a need.
Your Word further states in III John 2, "*Beloved, I wish above all things that thou mayest prosper and be in health, even as thy soul prospereth.*"
I am not prospering when I can't meet my obligations.
Father, your Word also states in Mark 11:24, "*Therefore I say unto you, What things soever you desire, when ye pray, believe that ye receive them, and ye shall have them.*"

Based on your Word, I claim $500 to pay my property taxes. It is both a need and a desire. According to Mark 11:24, I now believe that I receive my $500 to pay these taxes. I thank you for it, Father, in the name of Jesus. Amen.

C. THE PRAYER: (THANKSGIVING AND CONFESSION)

Father,
I thank you and praise you for my $500.
I believe that I have received it and I have it now.

From the moment you make your prayer of claiming the promise of God, you NEVER pray that prayer AGAIN. You never ask God for it again. You have made a claim by faith. You don't see the thing you prayed for yet in the physical realm. It has not yet been manifested to your senses. You have it by FAITH.

Hebrews 11:1 tells us, *"Now faith is the substance of things hoped for, the EVIDENCE of THINGS NOT SEEN."*

Faith becomes your evidence of the $500 you have claimed according to the Word of God. Continue to pray the prayer of confession and thanksgiving until the $500 materializes.

If you are truly acting in faith, you will wait with patience and confidence until the $500 comes. Then you'll say, "Thank you, Father, I have it." And that ends that transaction.

Before you actually see the $500 you say, "Thank you, Father. I believe that I've received my $500." Remember again Mark 11:24 said, *". . . WHEN you pray, BELIEVE that ye RECEIVE, and ye SHALL have them."*

If you really believe that you have received your need or desire, there is no need to ask for it again. To ask again is to say by the asking that you did not receive it when you prayed. To ask again for the same thing is to nullify your faith. To pray again would be to pray in doubt, and God cannot respond to doubt. He is a faith God, and it is faith that pleases Him, not doubt.

Don't let well-meaning friends or relatives pray for the $500 any more. By faith it is already done. If they want to pray, tell them to join with you in praying the prayer of confession and thanksgiving, because you already believe you have it.

Understand also that different people are at different stages of spiritual growth and development. Sometimes people who have not heretofore been exposed to this kind of teaching are weak and infantile in their faith of life. They hear this kind of teaching and it thrills them so that they want to go right out and start believing for *dollar bills*, when in fact, at that point in their faith life, they only have *ten-cent* faith. And because they try to believe for more than their faith can actually handle at any given point in their faith development, they become discouraged and give up the whole project.

Don't try to believe beyond your measure of faith. You can find out easily where it is. Simply ask yourself the question: "What can I believe God for?"

Notice I didn't say, "What can you believe God can do?" Most people would say, "I believe God can do anything." The issue at hand is not what God can do, but what can you believe Him for. In other words, can you believe Him for a dime or a dollar? For a Volkswagen or a Rolls Royce? For a Piper Cub or a "747"?

Can you stand on it and wait with patience and cool confidence even if it takes a year to manifest? You see, it's not a matter of God holding it back from you, but a matter of your faith producing the reality of it in your life.

Don't try to believe for a million dollars when you only have ten dollar faith. Learn to apply the faith principles on small things, then move up the ladder to bigger things. No one climbs a ladder by starting out on the top rung.

Start out by believing God for your next pair of socks or stockings. Anybody can use a charge plate or credit card. And I don't mean that there's anything wrong with that. I do think it takes more faith to believe God than it does to say, "Charge it." Start believing for socks or stockings and soon you will be believing for the shoes. Next it will be pants, shirts, coats, and then suits.

Often people who hear these teachings are already buried under 20 years of indebtedness and other assorted problems and want instant deliverance. And they'll pray —not really in faith—but in desperation. Fear of losing the house, fear of losing the car, and other fears enter in and nullify their faith.

But aside from all these things—faith works! And if you'll begin to purpose in your heart that you're going to *walk by faith and not by sight* (II Corinthians 5:7), God will most certainly honor His Word in your life.

The illustration we've given concerning the use of the principles of faith relative to finances, will work for every other area of your life—a new house, car, job, furniture, etc., etc. The principle works the same way. If you'll utilize the rules we've given, you will be an overcomer in your daily life.

Remember this important fact, however, no rule or principle is learned and perfected overnight. This is where the fruit of patience is developed, in the interim period from the time you make your claim on the promises of God, until it is physically and visibly manifested in your experience.

If you'll start out small—believing for small things which don't require *great* faith—you will soon be believing for great things and your faith will grow correspondingly. That's how faith grows—by using it—by claiming the promises of God's Word and standing on them until their physical fulfillment.

How To Receive Healing

Let's deal now with something which affects our physical bodies. *How to receive healing for your body by faith.*

A. FIND THE SCRIPTURES WHICH PROMISE YOU HEALING.

Again, every claim we make must be based on the written Word of God. A faith claim only has validity when it is grounded in the scriptures. Some examples of scriptures on healing are: Matthew 8:17; Mark 16:17-18; Mark 11:24; I Peter 2:24. These are not the only scriptures in the Bible on healing, but just a representative few.

B. THE PRAYER: (THE CLAIMING OF THE PROMISE OF GOD, RELATIVE TO YOUR HEALING.)

Heavenly Father,
I thank you for your Word.
Based on your Word which declares in Matthew 8:17, *"That it might be fulfilled which was spoken by Esaias the prophet, saying, Himself took our infirmities, and bare our sicknesses."*—

And I Peter 2:24 which says, *"Who his own self bare our sins in his own body on the tree, that we, being dead to sins, should live unto righteousness: by whose stripes ye were healed."*—

Father, according to these verses of scripture, Jesus *took* and *bore* my sicknesses and diseases, and with His stripes I *was* healed. *Took, bore,* and *was* (were) are all past tense terms, indicating the time of the action has already taken place as far as you are concerned.

Your Word further declares in Mark 11:24, *"What things soever ye desire, when ye pray, believe that ye receive them, and ye shall have them."*

You said, *"What things sover ye desire . . ."* I desire to be healed. I desire that this cancer leave my body.

You said, *". . . when ye pray . . ."* I am now praying.

You said, *". . . believe that ye receive them . . ."* I now believe that I receive my healing for this cancer. (Or, heart trouble, bad eyes, bad back, bad heart, etc.)

You said, *". . . and ye shall have them."* I believe I receive by faith. And faith is my evidence according to Hebrews 11:1, *"Now faith is . . . the evidence of things not seen."* By faith I have it. Therefore, it must come.

Thank you, Father, in Jesus' name. I believe I am healed.

C. THE PRAYER: (THANKSGIVING AND CONFESSION)

Father,
I thank you in Jesus' name.
I believe I have received my healing.
I believe that I have it now.

This prayer is to be prayed until the physical manifestation of the healing takes place in your body. Remember you are healed by faith and not by sight. Faith is your evidence of the healing, not the fact that the cancer has left your body. Your confession—between the time you pray and claim your healing until it is seen in your body—is what causes it to come. This is *faith healing,* simply believing you have received the healing because the Word of God says that *with His stripes you were healed.*

If you really believe that you are healed, you can see how unbelieving it would be to pray for that healing again. To pray again would be saying that you didn't get it the first time. Because if you did get it the first time, there would be no need to pray the second time. Right?

Now, your body may scream louder than ever that you are sick. Fever. Pain. Nausea. Lumps. Etc., etc. This is where your confession comes in. You must confess the Word of God in the face of every symptom and every pain. This is faith versus sense knowledge.

Remember that Satan is the god of this world, which includes everything in the sense realm. If you allow your faith to be affected by your senses, you will be defeated in every encounter of life. If, on the other hand, you allow your faith to be governed only by God's Word, you can be nothing less than a winner! Praise God!

Satan will shoot a pain to your body, and then a
thought to your mind suggesting that you are still sick.
At this point what you confess with your mouth will determine what you will have. (Mark 11:23) Confess the
pain and symptoms, and that will give Satan the legal
right to enforce it upon you. Confess what the Word of
God says about your condition, and you will have that.
Confess healing, and you will have it.

"Brother Price, if I say I feel well when in fact I feel
bad, wouldn't I be telling a lie?"

You are absolutely right. If you said you feel well
when in fact you feel bad, that would be telling a lie. But
I'm not saying for you to confess that you feel good when
you feel bad. I'm saying you are to confess what the
Word says, not what you feel.

Is God a liar?

Certainly not!

Well, He's the one who said it. I didn't. He's the one
who said that *with His stripes ye WERE healed.*

God is telling you that you were healed. Your body is
telling you that you are sick. Who are you going to believe? Whichever one you confess is what you'll have.

We are not saying, as some would tell you, that there
is no sickness and disease, that it's all a state of mind.
That's a lie of Satan to deceive you. If there was no such
thing as sickness and disease, don't you think God, of all
people, would know that?

Yet He said that Jesus took our infirmities and bore
our sicknesses. (Matthew 8:17) How could that be true
if sickness doesn't exist?

We're not saying sickness is not real. We're not saying
pain is not real. We're not talking about what we see or
feel, only about what we believe. If I believe what the
Word of God says and confess that with my mouth, then
I am not lying, but telling the truth, the whole truth, and
nothing but the truth.

Right in the face of pain, confess and believe that
you are healed. You're making a confession of faith at
that time, and not a confession of physical, visible fact. If
somebody asks you how you feel, don't tell them. You're

not under obligation to tell anybody how you feel. Confess only what you believe, not what you feel.

Suppose someone says, "How do you feel? You certainly don't look very well."

You may be feeling terrible. Don't tell them you feel good if you feel bad. Instead, confess and tell them what you believe. Say, "Praise God, the Word of God says in I Peter 2:24 that with His stripes I was healed. And in II Corinthians 5:7, it says that we walk by faith and not by sight. So, according to the Word of God, I believe that I am healed and I'm doing fine. How about you?"

At that point, you are not lying. You are telling the truth according to the Word of God. Now, when the physical evidence comes—the cancer disappears, the eyesight clears up, the tumor vanishes, etc.—then you can say, "I am healed." Until the physical evidence comes your confession should be, "I believe I am healed, examine the Word of God, it proves I am." When the physical evidence comes, you can say, "I am healed—examine my body—it proves it."

What About Medication?

"When I pray and make my claim to physical healing —until the physical evidence comes—should I continue to take my medication?"

Before I answer that, let me ask you these questions. Does wearing glasses heal bad eyes? Does taking insulin heal diabetes? Does taking glycerin heal a heart condition? Does taking dialysis heal kidneys?

You know as well as I do that the answer to all these questions is no. Wearing glasses doesn't heal bad eyes. If it did all you'd have to do is wear glasses. You wouldn't even have to pray. But it doesn't work like that. Wearing glasses, taking glycerin, taking insulin, will not heal anything and is therefore irrelevant and immaterial to your healing.

Whether you take the medication or not has nothing at all to do with your healing, unless, of course, your faith is in the medication. If it is, and you stop taking it, then you are in serious trouble.

Remember that you are receiving your healing by *faith*. It is a matter of what you believe in your *heart,* or *spirit.* Your *heart,* by *faith,* knows that you are healed, but your *body* doesn't know it yet. Therefore, your *body* may still need the medication. So go ahead and take it *if you need it.* All glasses and medication are doing is allowing the body to function at a normal level, until the physical healing is manifested in your body.

Now understand, if you had a healing manifested in your body and you continued in the face of that healing to take the medication, then that would be a denial of your healing and would open the door for Satan and demons to put the same thing on you—or something worse. If you are in fact healed, you don't need any medication, do you?

But, while you are making a stand in faith, your body may still need the medication. And thank God it is available. Don't get in bondage—take the medication *if you need it.* If you *can* do without it, that's even better. For it will allow you to put your confidence in your faith instead of the medication.

When *gifts of healings* operate, or miracle healings, as they are sometimes referred to, they are usually instantaneous. Therefore, there is no further need for glasses, crutches, wheelchairs, insulin, etc. But *faith healing* is different. Most of the time there can be a time factor between the time you pray and the time the physical evidence comes, and you may need the medication. *If you do,* take it. It is not a denial of your faith.

After all, remember that you have received your healing according to God's Word, not according to not taking medication. Many make the mistake of trying to prove faith healing is true by not taking medication, instead of by the clearly revealed Word of the Living God.